T0094722

The Autistic Holocaust

The reason why our children keep getting sick

Jon E. Mica

Published by:
Trine Day LLC
PO Box 577
Walterville, OR 97489
1-800-556-2012
www.TrineDay.com
publisher@TrineDay.net

Library of Congress Control Number: 2015936816

Mica, Jon E.
The Autistic Holocaust: The reason why our children keep getting
sick—1st ed.
p. cm.
Epud (ISBN-13) 978-1-937584-84-9
Mobi (ISBN-13) 978-1-937584-85-6
Print (ISBN-13) 978-1-937584-83-2
1. Autism in children -- Etiology. 2. Autistic Disorder -- etiology
-- Popular Works. 3. Vaccination of children -- Complications
-- United States. 4. Vaccines industry -- Corrupt practices --
United States. 5. Mercury -- adverse effects -- United States. I.
Mica, Jon E.. II. Title

FIRST EDITION
10 9 8 7 6 5 4 3 2 1

Printed in the USA
Distribution to the Trade by:
Independent Publishers Group (IPG)
814 North Franklin Street
Chicago, Illinois 60610
312.337.0747
www.ipgbook.com

This book is dedicated to my son Jon. He is the catalyst by which all this came to be. A wonderful young man descriptive beyond words or title. I love you son ...

Contents

CHAPTER ONE

MY ODYSSEY BEGINS

The United States is currently in the midst of an autistic holocaust. One 1 in 68 American children are autistic. If someone had told me two years ago that I would write a book – let alone a book on autism – I would have responded with amusement. Unfortunately, writing this book has largely been devoid of mirth, because my son is autistic.

I should warn the reader that this is not a heartwarming story of a family who discovers that their child has a neurological disorder with the benefit of an early diagnosis. This is also not a story of a close-knit family who overcomes misfortune by sticking together in love. Although this book doesn't have a storyline that would fit comfortably into a Lifetime movie, it has a Hollywood ending of sorts, because over the course of my journey to understand autism I have been reunited with both my father and my son.

My son, Jonny, came into the world on Saturday, August 23rd, 1986. It was sunny summer August morning, and earlier in the day there were no obvious signs that my wife, Carrie, would be entering labor. But the call came in around 9:30 A.M. from Crouse Irving Memorial Hospital in Syracuse, New York. At the time, I was a salesman at a car dealership, and I sped from the dealership to the hospital in about ten minutes. My mind was racing a thousand miles an hour as I drove to the hospital.

Hospital personnel instructed me to change into blue scrubs, and they ushered me into an operating room, where Carrie was being prepped for a Caesarean. Shoulder length brown hair framed her beautiful face that was slightly contorted by fear, and concern emanated from her usually glistening green eyes. She was lying on an operating table directly in front of me – just out of arms reach. A large bluish sheet covered her body from the neck down, and the doctors and nurses encircling Carrie were in the same blue scrubs that I wore, which were color coordinated with the sheet draping my wife. I thought it was a nice touch.

Although the operating room was a staccato whirlwind of activity, every movement unfolded in slow motion to me. My head was light, and my palms were sweating. I could feel adrenaline surging through my limbs. The butterflies in my stomach were beginning to migrate north to the back of my throat, making it hard to swallow. I nervously looked down at my wingtip shoes, admiring the shine from the previous day's polish. A sagacious older man once told me that you can learn a lot about a man by the appearance of his shoes. I don't necessarily know if that's the case, but since then, the appearance of my footwear has been a major concern for me.

By 10:41 A.M., the events of the morning – from my breakfast to the choice of my white and black, diamond speckled Van Heusen tie – were a series of lightening quick montages that flashed though my mind. The constant pressure of work's production quotas were also taking a backseat to the present moment, and I felt an indescribable elation.

At 10:42 A.M., forty pounds of fluid gushed out of Carrie and cascaded onto the operating room's tiled floor, and in the midst of the deluge was my six-pound son. I mustered the strength to walk over to my son. Drawing near him, I was nearly blinded by a glowing radiance that emulated from Carrie as she gently cradled him in her arms.

The look she cast at me that moment is forever etched in my memory. Truthfully, it was the single most sincere look of transparent love I'd ever seen from Carrie. It was so pure, so genuine, and earnestly gracious. Our miracle had arrived, and my attention quickly turned to my son. He appeared to be perfectly normal and healthy. He was a real heartbreaker, with a tuft of brown hair on the top of his precious little crown. My index finger filled his near translucent baby hand. The best moment of my life had come and gone. I was now a father!

Shortly after the miracle of Jonny's birth, the life that Carrie and I had forged for ourselves reverted back to its status quo as Carrie returned to her job. My mother enthusiastically served as a babysitter, and our close friends were more than happy to fill in the necessary vacancies. Our first Christmas as a family was wonderful. Throughout the drive to Carrie's parents, Jonny never cried. In fact, he never cried during his first year of his life, but I never thought it was odd, because I was new to fatherhood.

Our little family had all the hallmarks of a Norman Rockwell painting. Carrie and I ostensibly had a happy marriage, and we treasured our tender newborn. We both logged long hours to support the never-ending need for diapers, food, clothing, etc. As I logged long hours at work, I had the self-deluded perception that the car dealership needed my presence every single minute of every day. My wife and I also started to have frequent rows. At the time, I had no idea that I was falling into the abyss of an undiagnosed bipolar disorder, and my world was on the verge of imploding.

The long hours at work cycled into manic episodes. I would be awake for two or three days, and then sleep for hours due to sheer exhaustion. I distinctly recall coming home early one evening to cover for Carrie, as she was called into work unexpectedly. I was dead tired. After preparing dinner for Jonny and I, we snuggled into bed. It felt great to have his little body next to mine, and we peacefully drifted off to sleep.

My sound reverie was suddenly shattered. I was shaken violently from a deep sleep by Carrie, who returned home early and found Jonny asleep in the living room. As I was sleeping, he had found the energy to navigate his way down the hall and onto the soft comforts of the living room carpet. But not before he had successfully managed to turn on every single burner on the gas stove in the kitchen.

Our marriage had become rife with friction, and that night proved to be the critical mass in the demise of our relationship. I don't blame Carrie in the least for leaving, even though both of us shared culpability in the end of our marriage. Within a year, we were separated by two counties, but enjoying the comforts of a new life and better relationships.

Two years after our divorce was finalized, I remarried to a remarkable woman thirteen years my senior. Linda was equally lovely on the inside and the outside, and she also embraced Jonny into her heart. Carrie remarried too, and she became Jonny's primary care giver. His visitations with Linda and I were on a weekly basis. Although the time we spent with him was blissful, I watched my son incrementally developing in weekend frames over the ensuing years.

At Jonny's birth and throughout his first year, he was administered all his recommended scheduled vaccinations. Unfortunately, at the time, I didn't have an inclination that the vaccinations were possibly a factor in his unusually slow development, social handicaps, and reserved verbal expressions. I resigned myself to the fact that my son was different than other children his age.

Jonny was medium height but very thin. He had sandy blond hair and sparkling blue eyes. He was slower in comprehension and application of skills when compared to his cousins, and his ability to converse was awkward at times and short in duration. He also seemed to be emotionally flat-lined. Despite Jonny's salient social disadvantages, I encouraged him to be more outgoing, more vocal, and more involved in life. We shared in the all the normal past times that are shared by fathers and sons, but we squeezed them into one weekend at a time.

Linda's brother, Jeff, had three children, who Jonny played with whenever he visited. Jeffery, Jr., was approximately Jonny's age, and he was followed chronologically by Scotty and Gabriel. Jeffery was a remarkably astute five-year-old and tall for his age. He had dark brown hair and enthusiastic brown eyes that were magnified by his thick glasses. He had several visible developmental advantages over my own son. Plus, he had no self-reservations, and all of his problem solving and social interaction skills seemed to come natural.

Whenever Jonny and Jeffery were together, it was Jeffery who assumed the role of an older loving and caring brother. And, yes, older brothers often like to play tricks on their younger brothers. Years later Jonny would disclose to me that Jeffery handed him a piece of a "Bazooka Joe-like" substance, passing it off as gum, which, much to Jonny's dismay, turned out to be Silly Putty!

I would probably venture to guess that there were other practical jokes Jeffrey would devise at Jonny's expense, but they had a loving bond. In fact, it was Jonny's only bond with someone his age. Jeffery was both Jonny's teacher and friend. Even at a young age, I believe he was insightful enough to draw the same conclusions about my son's condition, and he was careful not to offend him.

I have no doubts that Jonny enjoyed playing with Jeffery, but, given the choice, the quality time he spent with me took precedent. We enjoyed the hour-long car rides from my place to Carrie's new house in Oswego County. I sang and Jonny would nervously smile and listen, occasionally throwing in the well timed "Ohh-aah, Ohh-aah" to my rendition of Sam Cooke's "Chain Gang." I would sing primarily to dispel the silence, because Jonny was rather taciturn. And we always enjoyed ice cream cones after a round of miniature golf.

The duplex I shared with Linda bordered several acres of undeveloped woodlands and marsh, which doubled as a wildlife sanctuary. Deer, owls, raccoons, and every known species of fowl indigenous to our region of upstate New York were frequent fixtures in our backyard. Jonny enjoyed our home and location as much as we did – especially the towering maple tree in our back yard, which anchored a sturdy, old fashion homemade tire swing. Growing grass never stood a chance in the path of the swing. The time tested dirt path of the swing remains until this day, twenty years after Jonny's last push. In the late fall, the tree provided a mountainous pile of leaves that swallowed Jon and Jeffery as they took turns diving into it. Those two never got cold, so we monitored them through the comforts of the kitchen window.

Although Jonny was extremely reserved, the question of what he wanted for his eighth birthday elicited a wellspring of emotion. His eyes popped wide open and his eyebrows raised, and a deaf person would've easily deciphered his enthusiastic response: "I want Super Mario Brothers!" In 1994, the Super Mario Brothers video game was about $300, which presented a slight financial challenge for me. But not fulfilling his birthday wish wasn't an option. I became a superstar in Jonny's gleaming eyes as he opened his birthday present. I'm severely electronically challenged, so it took an interminable afternoon to hook up Super Mario Brothers. Hours elapsed as Jon watched in hopeful anticipation, clutching his control panel, and I whispered silent expletives. Then, suddenly, I shouted: "Game-on!"

I was quite relieved after the video game was operational, but an unexpected phenomenon quickly unfolded right before my eyes. As Jonny slipped deeper and deeper into the video game, our social interaction was immediately suspended. The game became an obsession instead of a form of entertainment. Linda's brother also had a Super Mario Brothers, and our visits to his house afforded Jonny the opportunity to further hone his skills. Jeffery had no problems mastering the successively more difficult levels of play in short order, but Jonny was stuck on the same level. It was painful to watch. My suspicions of his developmental delay were being confirmed weekend after weekend.

Linda's brother purchased a farm on the outskirts of Syracuse, and it was stocked with horses, goats, chickens, rams, pigs, and sheep. I brought Jonny out to the farm, and Jonny tagged behind Jeffery and I followed in their wake. When we walked by the ad hoc petting zoo, Jonny started repeating the same statement over and over. "Hey, what's that green stuff?"

I always wanted to shield my son from any embarrassment, and I would explain away his deficiencies whenever possible, but I had difficulties covering for him as Jeffery's father started to chide Jonny. Although I was fuming, I didn't want to cause a scene, so I quelled my fury. Jonny's repetitious chant started falling off gradually, and the volume turned down too. After our tour of the ad hoc petting zoo, Jeffery and his dad started to shoot cans off an old wooden fence with a .22 rifle. Jonny requested to shoot the rifle, and I closely supervised him as he shot at a bale of hay. After I drove Jonny back to Carrie's, he told her that he had shot a rifle, and she was livid. In fact, I think if she had had a gun, she would've shot me on the spot.

Carrie's amicability sharply declined after our visit to the farm, and we then had several squabbles over child support, because my undiagnosed bipolar disorder was making me increasingly dysfunctional, and I found it extremely difficult to hold onto jobs and maintain my child support payments, which ignited arguments between Carrie and me.

Carrie took me to court on a few occasions due to my child support arrears. One morning, I showed up to court in response to a court summons. I thought the summons was about child support arrears, but after arriving in court, I discovered Carrie and her attorney were springing adoption proceedings on me. Carrie had primed Jonny to testify that I was less than an optimal father. I looked at the acute discomfort and anguish on Jonny's face, and I made a spur of the moment decision: I didn't want to subject Jonny to testifying, so I acquiesced to the adoption proceedings. The judge said, "This is the most selfless thing I've ever seen anyone do." I truly thought I was acting in my son's best interest, but aside from my mother's death, it was the most emotionally devastating day of my life.

Jonny's adoption proceedings in 1995 officially welcomed him into his new family, and it also marked a turning point in the severity of both of our disorders. My bipolar disorder became progressively pronounced and painful. I was first diagnosed in with bipolar disorder in 1997, during a brief period of institutionalization, and I was institutionalized again in 1999.

Although Linda hung in there with me throughout this difficult period, my reality descended into a lightless abyss of depression as the vestiges of stability vanished from my life. My calls and letters to Jonny received no responses. In 2000, however, when Jonny was fourteen years old, I achieved a modicum of stability and I reconnected with him via emails. I discovered that Jonny had been diagnosed with Asperger syndrome, which was one of the five disorders that comprise the "*autism spectrum disorder*" *or ASD*. He had been removed from school in the tenth grade, because of his severe emotional and social handicaps. He even attempted suicide and had been institutionalized for a short period of time.

I love my son, and I wouldn't want to change him for all the money in the world – or change anyone for that matter. We all have flaws and imperfections, and we all desperately want to be loved for who we are. We are all blessed in different ways, including our shortcomings. But as I struggled with bipolar disorder, I felt helpless, confused, and partially responsible for my son's condition. Grief and guilt compelled me to roll up my sleeves and educate myself on every aspect of autism. I quickly learned that children whose parents have been diagnosed with bipolar disorder or schizophrenia are at a much greater risk of acquiring autism, which only served to exacerbate my guilt.

CHAPTER TWO

MY DAD REVISITED

I graduated from high school in 1977, and my formal education ceased at that point. My dad, the scientist, on the other hand, is sharp as a tack, and he often boasts that a couple of his patented innovations saved General Electric millions of dollars. Though my dad excels at probability, statistics, and science, he is assuredly lacking in humility. But I certainly admire his accomplishments, both past and present, and without his influence this book wouldn't have been written.

At times, common sense isn't so common to my dad, even though he could probably explain quantum physics to a child. My dad's shirts were invariably equipped with a plastic pocket protector that contained no less than three pens and a slide rule, and activism comes naturally to him. When I was growing up in the township of Clay, New York, we lived near Onondaga Lake, which may have been one of the most polluted lakes in America. Over the years, Allied Chemical had dumped millions of gallons of toxic waste into the lake. The mercury content of the lake was extremely high, and the fish that survived the lake probably retained more mercury than a thermometer. One day, while at the lake, my dad sprung into action. He posted a sign that was filled with expletives, which I won't repeat. It's my first memory of my dad taking a stand.

Dad took great pleasure in assisting me during high school social studies assignments. He would dictate, and I would write. Thanks to dad I always scored a 100 percent, even though, I have to confess, I couldn't understand what the hell he told me to wrote most of the time. Over all, he meant well, and he was a pretty good father, but he also had a dark side. He was the consummate disciplinarian, and the entire family often walked on eggshells in his majestic presence. My sisters and I have a number of very painful memories growing up. A leather belt to the fanny generally wasn't his modus operandi, even though he administered it occasionally. My dad was more inclined to discipline his children with pushups, squat thrusts, and sit-ups.

My mom and dad were divorced when I was 18 in 1977. My sisters and I were probably happier about the divorce than even my mother. I hadn't seen my dad since 1977 when he visited Linda and me in 1990. When he showed up at our house, I could see that he had aged, but he still possessed the energy of two people. He had a thick head of shortly cropped brown hair, and he was about six feet tall. He wore a blue button down shirt, blue jeans, and slightly worn black dress shoes. Over the preceding years, my dad had acquired a hefty paunch. My dad arrived with his customary charm, but his charm could switch to scorn in a heartbeat.

In 2011, I managed to locate dad though peoplefinders.com, and we embarked on a snail mail correspondence before actually speaking on the phone. We hadn't spoken in 21 years. My dad reminds me of a character out of the *Peanuts* comic strip – Snoopy's Uncle Spike. Maybe my dad didn't speak to cacti like Uncle Spike, but if dad had any friends they were a secret to me. Uncle Spike appeared infrequently in his nephew's life, and he always appeared when least expected. My dad was like that too.

He had been an engineer with General Electric for 22 years when he was laid off, and he attributed the loss of his job to the North American Free Trade Agreement. Since he left General Electric, my dad had worn several existential hats over the years: he had been a consultant, video producer, and a part-time school bus driver. As a school bus driver, he interacted with several children who had been diagnosed with autism, and he realized that something was seriously awry due to seemingly exponential proliferation of autism.

My dad has proven to be quite instrumental in helping me investigate the current autism epidemic and God bless him. He began to mail me books on autism that I devoured. The first book on autism that he sent me was *Sacred Spark*, which was written by a United Methodist minister, Reverend Lisa K. Sykes. Her son, Wesley, had been diagnosed with autism, and she concluded that his autism was the result of mercury poisoning via a vaccine. I then wondered if it were possible that my son's neurological impairments could have been the resultant effect of vaccines.

My dad ultimately decided to include me in his grand plans. His expertise in electronics and computers enabled him to segue into Internet broadcasting, and he developed an Internet television network. Dad was editing and broadcasting weekly shows through United Christian Counseling in Indiana 24/7 on tvunetworks.com. He eventually suggested that I host one of the shows. The latter suggestion sounded appealing to me, even though it filled me with trepidation, because it was far afield of my prior life experiences, and I was still struggling with my bipolar disorder. The duration of the shows were 15 minutes, and their primary focus was autism and other neurological disorders. I ultimately overcame my initial fears and accepted his offer.

The channel was broadcasting around the clock, even though it wasn't exactly providing competition for major television networks, but we had viewers in 54 countries. The network focused a great deal of its attention on the autism epidemic. Dad was enthusiastic about the undertaking, because somebody, somewhere was tuned into our broadcasts, and it was the content of our broadcasts that mattered for him. I believed in the content too.

Prior 2011, I had merely scratched the surface of autism and its various manifestations and etiologies. Still, I was excited at the proposition of sharing my burgeoning knowledge on autism with our audience. Along the way, I encountered some well-known scientists and world-class activists, who shared common beliefs about the current autism epidemic, and whose names and research are contained in this book.

CHAPTER THREE

THE AUTISTIC HOLOCAUST

Prior to 2013, Autistic Spectrum Disorder (ASD) was an amalgam of five neurodevelopmental disorders that include autism disorder, *pervasive developmental disorder*, Asperger syndrome, childhood disintegrative disorders, and Rett's syndrome. The Diagnostic and Statistical Manual of Mental Disorders (DSM), published by the American Psychiatric Association, is the standard for the classification of mental disorders, and it first included autism as a distinct diagnostic category in 1980. The DSM-III (the third edition of the DSM) noted that a central feature of "infantile autism" was a pervasive developmental disorder, and two-thirds of infants afflicted by it would remain severely handicapped and unable to lead independent lives.

In the United States, autism in proliferating at unprecedented rates – 14% annually. It has a greater prevalence than childhood cancer, juvenile diabetes, and pediatric AIDS combined. Indeed, according to the No Child Left Behind Act and the Individuals with Disabilities Education Act, ASD is proliferating at a much greater rate than all other developmental disorders combined. In 1999, the California Department of Developmental Services reported a 273 percent jump in the number of children being treated for autism between 1987 and 1998 in the state. In 2002, the U.S. Department of Education reported that nationwide autism rates had jumped 556 percent in a decade.

The Harvard School of Public Health published a study in 2006, estimating the lifetime cost of care for one child with autism is $3.2 million, and that it costs society an estimated $35 billion each year to care for all individuals with autism.[1] But there are also experts in the field that believe $3.2 million is an extremely conservative estimate. The case of Hanna Poling gives an indication that the lifetime costs of autism significantly eclipse $3.2 million. Hannah Poling was normal, happy, and precocious in her first 18 months of life, but after being vaccinated against nine diseases in one doctor's visit, she developed ASD. The Office of Special Masters of the US Federal Claims Court, which adjudicates vaccine injury claims, awarded her family $1.5 million for her care and the additional complications she accrued due to her ASD in her first year of life, and her family will also receive more than $500,000 yearly to pay for Hannah's care. Her compensation could easily exceed $20 million over her lifetime. If Hanna's compensation is closer to reality than the government estimate, and her $20 million reward is multiplied by the ever-increasing number of children diagnosed with autism, the price tag for ASD will be in the trillions in the not so distant future.

Lisa Joyce is not a scientist or doctor; she's the mother of an autistic child. She is also a blogger, author, and autism advocate. One of the common denominators of many people who have issues with the recommended vaccination schedules is that they are parents of vaccine-injured children. Lisa Joyce collected over 40 scientific studies that supported an association between vaccinations and neurological disorders such as autism.

One study, conducted at the Stony Brook University Medical Center in New York, evaluated the association between the hepatitis B vaccination of male neonates and parental reports of ASD.[2] The study found that boys who received the hepatitis B vaccine during the first month of life had a three-

1   archive.sph.harvard.edu/press-releases/2006-releases/press04252006. html.

2   Gallagher C.M., Goodman M.S. Hepatitis B vaccination of male neonates and autism diagnosis, NHIS 1997-2002. J Toxic of Environ Health A. 2010; 73(24): 1655-77. PMID: 21058170.

fold greater risk of developing ASD, and the risk was greatest for non-Caucasian boys.

In addition to ASD, vaccines can have serious side effects, including paralysis and death. A significant number of sudden infant death syndrome (SIDS) cases have occurred shortly after an infant has received vaccinations. Moreover, SIDS accounts for approximately half the deaths that are reported to the Vaccine Adverse Event Reporting System (VAERS), a national vaccine safety surveillance program co-sponsored by the CDC and the Food and Drug Administration (FDA) that contains information on unverified reports of adverse events following immunization with US-licensed vaccines. (The VAERS data is often criticized, because anyone can submit a VAERS report at www.vaers.hhs.gov. A majority of VAERS reports are filed by vaccine manufacturers (37%), and health care providers (36%). State immunization programs account for (10%), vaccine recipients or their parents or guardians account for seven percent, other sources-ten percent.[3] Only about one percent of serious adverse events (SAE) are reported to the FDA.[4]) Unfortunately, as this story unfolds, the reader will realize that the CDC and FDA have been less than forthcoming about the deleterious effects of vaccines.

Many readers of this book will no doubt be skeptical of my thesis that vaccinations are inextricably linked to autism. The government, however, has been less than candid about vaccines and their potential for harm, starting with the polio vaccine. So before embarking on a discussion of contemporary vaccines and autism, I will discuss the realities surrounding the great myth of Jonas Salk's polio vaccine.

Jonas Salk is a great American hero, because his polio vaccine eradicated polio in the U.S., right? Wrong. Dr. Albert Sabin developed the vaccine that was largely responsible for eradicating polio in the U.S. Teasing out the myth from the reality regarding the polio vaccine would require a book onto itself, but for the purposes of this book, I'll give a truncated overview of the Salk-Sabine controversy.

---

3   http://vaers.hhs.gov/about/faqs#who_reports.
4   www.fda.gov/MedWatch/UCM201419.

On April 12ᵗʰ, 1955, the Foundation for Infantile Paralysis, which later morphed in the March of Dimes, told the world, using every possible means of publicity, that the vaccine invented by Dr. Jonas E. Salk was "safe, potent, and efficient." On that day, Dr. Thomas Francis, of the University of Michigan, who had been entrusted with the task of evaluating the Salk vaccine, issued his eagerly anticipated report on the 1954 tests of the vaccine. At a meeting of 500 doctors and scientists at Ann Arbor, Michigan, Dr. Salk and Dr. Francis made such sweeping claims for the vaccine that nearly every American newspaper declared that Dr. Salk had abolished polio. Even before the momentous announcement by Dr. Francis at Ann Arbor, six pharma companies had orders from the Foundation for Infantile Paralysis to manufacture enough vaccines to inoculate 9 million children and pregnant women. Two hours after the announcement by Drs. Francis and Salk, the government licensed the vaccine and released it for en masse distribution to children in the U.S.

Salk's vaccine was derived from monkeys who had the polio virus. After the monkeys' kidneys were surgically removed, they were sliced and diced into tiny pieces and deposited into glass bottles with a special nutrient solution devised by Dr. Salk. The glass bottles were then placed in an incubator to stimulate the growth of the kidney cells. Afterwards, the virus was killed by a formaldehyde solution. Although the virus in Salk's vaccine was killed by the formaldehyde solution, it imparted enough polio antibodies to surmount exposure to the disease, but children had to receive three vaccinations with the Salk vaccine plus a booster to be fully inoculated against the disease.

As the Salk vaccine was being administered to American children from coast-to-coast, Albert Sabine was developing a polio vaccine that was derived from an "attenuated" polio virus. The attenuated vaccine had a live but greatly weakened virus that wouldn't cause polio, but it nonetheless imparted enough polio antibodies to prevent polio. An additional benefit of the Sabin vaccine was that it was administered orally, eventually on a sugar cube, and it only had to be administered once, whereas Salk's vaccine schedule included four intramuscular injections.

Sabin maintained that Salk's vaccine was potentially dangerous, and he was an outspoken critic of it. But his warnings generally fell on deaf ears, because the Foundation for Infantile Paralysis and, for that matter, the government had put all of their chips on the Salk vaccine, so Sabine had to test his vaccine elsewhere, and Stalin's Soviet Union proved to be a willing participant. Between 1955 and 1961, Sabin's attenuated, oral vaccine was tested on at least 100 million people in the USSR, parts of Eastern Europe, Singapore, Mexico, and the Netherlands.

As Sabine was testing his vaccine in people who resided in the far reaches of the globe, Sabine's warnings about the Salk vaccine were proving to be prophetic, because of the "Cutter catastrophe." On April 24, 1955, just days after the Salk vaccine was lauded to save the world from polio, polio broke out among children who had received shots of the Salk vaccine made by Cutter Laboratories in California. A number of children contracted polio from the vaccine and at least eleven deaths are attributed to the Cutter catastrophe. It is speculated that the Cutter Laboratories hadn't properly killed the virus in its lots of vaccine, but the presence of the live virus has never been satisfactorily explained. After the Cutter catastrophe, research continued into alternatives to the Salk vaccine, and its production methods were changed.

By the early 1960s, the Sabin vaccine, which had shown its safety and efficacy in over 100 million people, was eventually adopted by the government as its polio vaccine of choice. It was cheaper to make and much cheaper and easier to administer – a single sugar cube versus multiple shots and a booster. So ultimately it was the Sabin vaccine that eradicated polio in the U.S. and not the Salk vaccine, even though most history books have overlooked the true facts about this matter.

In 1999, however, our government concluded that Sabin's vaccine causes polio in one out of every 2.4 million doses administered, so a modified Salk vaccine is now the polio vaccine of choice in the U.S., even though the Sabin vaccine is the predominant vaccine used for the rest of the world. It seems that our government is extremely sensitive in its protection of U.S. children if it's willing to replace an efficacious vaccine, because it induces polio in one of every 2.4 million children exposed to the vaccine, but, after reading the data I've collated for this book, the reader may very well wonder why the government isn't so sensitive on issues regarding vaccines and autism.

A postscript to both the Salk and Sabine vaccines is that both contained a human carcinogen – simian virus 40 (SV40) – until 1963, and SV40 was administered to millions of children via the Salk and Sabin vaccines. Multiple studies have shown that SV40 is a human carcinogen, and it has been found in various tumors, particularly mesothelioma, a malignant form of lung cancer, but the CDC disputes the fact that it causes cancer.

The CDC's earliest disavowals that human tumors containing SV40 were predicated on a study conducted by Howard Strickler who formerly served as a senior clinical investigator for the National Cancer Institute, which is a branch of the NIH, and Keerti Shah who's been a consultant for two big pharma vaccine concerns – Merck and Pfizer.[5] Their study reported that they hadn't found any evidence of SV40 in 50 samples of mesothelioma. Strickler posited that various laboratories that found SV40 in tumors had inadvertently contaminated the mesothelioma samples with SV40, which was rather unlikely.[6]

Researchers throughout the world were outraged by the findings of Stickler and Shah, because it categorically discounted their findings to the contrary. Finally, to settle the matter once and for all the International Mesothelioma Interest Group conscripted world-renowned geneticist Joseph Testa, who specializes in mesothelioma research,

5   Strickler H.D., et al. Contamination of poliovirus Vaccines with simian virus 40 (1955-1963) and subsequent cancer Rates. JAMA. 1998 Jan 28; 279(4): 292-5. PMID: 9450713.

6   Klein G., Powers A., Croce C., Association of SV40 with human tumors. Oncogene. 2002 Feb 14; 21(8): 1141-9. PMID: 11850833.

to conduct a study to determine whether or not SV40 was present in human mesothelioma tumors. Testa was skeptical of the claims that SV40 can cause or promote mesothelioma, because he thought that asbestos, an immune suppressant, was solely the culprit. But lo and behold, all four laboratories that participated in the Testa study found SV40 in at least nine out of the twelve mesothelioma samples they tested, and each laboratory's control samples tested negative, indicating that the positive SV40 samples were not the result of laboratory contamination. The results were published in the journal of *Cancer Research* in 1998.[7] The editor of *Cancer Research*, a member of the National Academy of Sciences, felt that Testa's results not only indisputably proved that SV40 is present in human tumors, but he said that SV40 is a contributing factor for mesothelioma.

Despite the fact that scores of researchers have found SV40 in mesothelioma tumors, the CDC maintains: "SV40 virus has been found in certain types of cancer in humans, but it has not been determined that SV40 causes these cancers." If the government conceded that SV40 in the polio vaccines from the 1950s and 1960s promoted or caused mesothelioma, its financial liability would potentially be enormous, so it's been unwavering in its denials.

Now, imagine, if the present day vaccines were causing autism. The liability for the government would be far greater than its liability for mesothelioma, so a government cover up makes sense – like the mesothelioma or, for that matter, the Agent Orange cover up. Indeed, this book will delineate the unethical and illegal lengths the government traverses to guard its secrets concerning autism.

---

7   Testa JR, et al. A multi-institutional study confirms the presence and expression of simian virus 40 in human malignant mesotheliomas. Cancer Research. 1998 Oct 15; 58(20): 4505-9 PubMed 9788590.

CHAPTER FOUR

QUICKSILVER FOR CHILDREN

As I mentioned earlier, *Sacred Spark*, a book written by the Reverend Lisa K. Sykes, was my wake up call regarding vaccines and autism. She felt her son's autism was due to mercury poisoning via vaccines. Numerous vaccines prior to 2000 contained the preservative thimerosal, which is 49.6 percent ethylmercury.

Many of us are familiar with the toxicity of mercury to a degree. Lewis Carroll's 1865 classic novel *Alice in Wonderland* brought notoriety to the Mad Hatter. During the 1800's, a mercury solution was commonly used in the process of turning fur into felt, and the phrase "Mad as a Hatter" was used to describe the condition of hatters or hat makers who were unwittingly exposed to mercury's highly toxic fumes.

Despite its extreme toxicity, mercury has played a role in medicine for centuries. In the 1920s, the diuretic properties of mercury were discovered, which resulted in "organomercurial diuretic therapy." Throughout the 1950s, mercury was a state-of-the-art diuretic. But when it was realized that death was a side effect of mercury the government decided that a difficulty urinating was preferable to death, so mercury diuretics were taken off the market.

In 1928, pharmaceutical giant Eli Lilly was first credited with the introduction of thimerosal, an ethylmercury containing preservative that's still used in vaccines. A year later,

Dr. K.C. Smithburn was treating patients with meningitis, and he injected 22 of them with thimerosal. Subsequently, researchers H.M. Powell and W.A. Jamieson published a study on thimerosal based on Dr. Smithburn's observations.[1] Powell and Jamieson's study, published in the September 1931 American Journal of Hygiene, stated that thimerosal had a "low order of toxicity" for humans, but Powell and Jamieson neglected to mention that all 22 of Dr. Smithburn's patients died of meningitis in the wake of receiving thimerosal, and seven died within a day of receiving thimerosal. A minor oversight, I guess. Unbelievably, the Powell and Jamieson study was used as evidence for the safety of thimerosal until 2002.

Since the 1930's, thimerosal has been used as a preservative in a number of vaccines and drugs to prevent contamination by harmful microbes, despite the fact that mercury has the potential to cause neuro-degeneration. In 1997, a team of research scientists demonstrated that mercury vapor inhalation by animals produced molecular legions in brain protein metabolism, which was similar to the legions seen in 80 percent of brains affected by Alzheimer's.[2] Studies conducted by scientists at the University of Calgary were published in NeroReport in 2001. Their research revealed direct evidence that mercury alters the cell membrane structure of developing neurons, and reveals evidence that mercury causes neuro-degeneration. More importantly, the study provided the first direct evidence that low-level mercury exposure is indeed a factor that can initiate neuro-degreneration within the brain.

A study published in May 2008 in the *Journal of Neurological Sciences*, supports an association between the mercury found in vaccinations and neurodevelopmental disorders and autism.[3] The study examined CDC supplied

---

1   Powell H.M., Jamieson W.A., Merthiolate as a Germicide. Am J Hyg. 1931; 13: 296-310.

2   Leong C.C., Syed N.I., Lorscheider F.L. Retrograde degeneration of neurite membrane structural integrity of nerve growth cones following in vitro exposure to mercury. NeuroReport. 2001 Mar 16; 12(4): 733-7. PMID: 11277574.

3   Young H.A., Geier D.A., Geier M.R. Thimerosal exposure in infants and

medical vaccination records of 278,624 infants from 1990 through 1996. Statistics showed a twofold to fourfold increase in ASD, tics, emotional disturbances, developmental and learning disorders, after exposure to an additional 100 micrograms of ethylmercury from vaccinations. The increase for autism was almost threefold greater.

A study published in *Neuroendocrinology Letters* in 2006 analyzed the VAERS database, and it compared the neurodevelopment disorders of children receiving the thimerosal-containing Diphtheria-Tetanus-acellular-Pertussis (DTaP) vaccines versus children receiving thimerosal-free DTaP vaccines between 1997 and 2000.[4] There were 57,151,417 vaccine doses administered to the children in the group exposed to thimerosal, and 47,985,230 vaccines to the children in the group who weren't exposed to thimerosal. The study's investigators concluded that mercury exposure had a significant affect on the incidence of autism, speech disorders, mental retardation, personality disorders, thinking abnormalities, ataxia, and neurodevelopmental disorders in general.

A study published in *Toxicological & Environmental Chemistry* in 2008 investigated the relationship between mercury exposure from the thimerosal containing hepatitis B vaccination in 1,824 children, whose ages ranged from 1 to 9 years of age, and their incidence of developmental disabilities based on an examination of data from the US CDC's 1999-2000 National Health and Nutrition Survey.[5] The study's researchers concluded that the odds of developmental disabilities were about nine times greater for boys receiving thimerosal-containing hepatitis B vaccinations than those who were unvaccinated.

neurodevelopmental disorders: an assessment of computerized medical records in the vaccine safety datalink. J Neurol Sci. 2008 Aug 15;27(1-2): 110-8. PMID: 18482737..

4   Geier D.A, Geier M.R. A meta-analysis epidemiological assessment of neurodevelopmental disorders following vaccines administered from 1994 through 2000 in the United States. Neuroendocrinol Lett. 2006; 27(4): 401-13 PMID: 16807526.

5   Gallagher C., Goodman M. Hepatitis B triple series vaccine and developmental disability in US children 1-9 years. Toxicology & Environmental Chemistry. 2008 Sep; 90(5): 997-1008.

A study conducted by researchers at the University of Texas assessed the affect of mercury in the environment and its correlation with autism, and they used data from the Environmental Protection Agency to gauge mercury release and autism data from the Texas Educational Agency.[6] The researchers found that for every 1,000 pounds of mercury released from industrial facilities and power plants there was a respective corresponding increase in autism. Distances to these sources of mercury were independent predictors of the autism increases, and for every 10 miles from industrial or power plant sources there was an associated decrease in the incidence in autism.

The reader might wonder whether or not these studies have validity, because mercury amalgam dental fillings have been used for decades, and people with these fillings aren't dropping dead like flies. True. But mercury body burden accumulates over a period of time until reaching a point of toxicity that manifests in disease. The International Academy of Oral Medicine and Toxicology released some cold, hard facts about the dangers of mercury filling amalgams.[7] Every time a person with mercury fillings eats or drinks a hot beverage, mercury vapors are released into their oral cavity, which are absorbed into their blood stream.[8] The vapors are odorless, colorless, and have no taste. The average person has three fillings and the potential to ingest mercury daily.[9]

6   Palmer RF, Blanchard S, Wood R. Proximity to point sources of environmental mercury release as a predictor of autism prevalence. Health Place. 2009 March; 15(1): 18-24. PMID: 18353703.
7   Kall J., et al. International Academy of Oral Medicine and Toxicology (IAOMT) position statement against dental mercury fillings for medical and dental practitioners, dental students, and practitioners. 2013 April 16: pg 2-52. iaomt.org/wp-content/uploads/IAOMT-2013-Position-Statement.pdf.
8   Lorscheider FL, Vimy MJ, Summers AO. Mercury exposure from "silver" tooth fillings: emerging evidence questions a traditional dental paradigm. Federation of American Societies for Experimental Biology (FASEB J.). 1995 April; 9(7): 504-8. PMID 7737458.
9   Vimy MJ, Lorscheider FL. Serial measurements of intra-oral air mercury: estimation of daily doses from dental amalgam. Journal on Dental Research (J Dental Res), 1985 August; 64(8):1072-5. PMID 3860539.

Experiments with monkeys[10] and sheep[11] with dental amalgams, show that mercury vapors released from chewing transfer to the placenta and to the fetuses body. Mercury levels increased in newborn lambs from drinking their mothers milk. Scientists have proven the same thing happens in humans. Swedish[12] and Brazilian[13] scientists have concluded that mercury from dental amalgams was the main source of mercury in breast milk.

Interestingly, not a single scientist on the FDA advisory panel on dental amalgams endorsed the 2009 FDA rule that promoted unrestricted mercury amalgam use in children and pregnant women. Again in 2010, the same panel recommended against the use of mercury amalgams in young children and women, but the FDA ignored its recommendations.

The FDA has been slow to embrace the dangers posed by mercury amalgam fillings, but Canada, Australia, Sweden, Denmark, and the United Kingdom have enacted measures protecting children and pregnant women from mercury amalgam fillings. Moreover, the fifth session of the Intergovernmental Negotiating Committee (INC5) convened in Geneva, Switzerland 2013 to prepare a global, legally binding directive on mercury. The delegates from more than 140 countries agreed on requirements to phase out mercury dental amalgams due to their toxicity. The INC5 also proposed the banning of a myriad of mercury containing products: batteries, compact florescent lamps, soaps, cosmetics, thermometers, and blood pressure measuring devices, dental amalgams, etc. Strangely enough, vaccines containing

---

10   Hahn L.J., et al. Whole body imaging of the distribution of mercury released from dental fillings into monkey tissues. FASEB J. 1994 Nov; 4(14): 3256-60. PMID: 2227216.

11   Vimy M.J., Tahkahashi Y., Lorscheider F.L., Maternal-fetal distribution of mercury (203 Hg) released from dental amalgam fillings. Am J Physiol. 1990 Apr; (4 pt 2): R939-45. PMID: 2331037.

12   Björnberg K.A., et al. Transport of methyl and inorganic mercury to the fetus and breast-fed infant. Environ Health Perspect. 2006 Oct; 113(10): 1381-5. PMCID: PMC1281284.

13   da Costa S.L., Malm O., Dorea J.G., Breast-fed milk mercury concentrations and amalgam surfaces in mothers from Brasila, Brazil. Biol Trace Elem Res. 2005 Aug; 106(2): 145-51. PMID: 16116246.

thimerosal were conspicuously absent from the mercury containing products that the INC5 proposed to ban.

The removal of thimerosal from most vaccines in the U.S. was mandated by the FDA's Modernization Act, which was signed into law on November 21, 1997. The amendment arose from long-standing concerns about lessening human exposure to mercury. But vaccine manufacturers weren't in a hurry to remove thimerosal from vaccines. In September 1999, Merck announced that its new line of vaccines were thimerosal free, but it continued to dispense the remainder of thimerosal-preserved vaccines. Merck finally ceased distributing its stockpiles of thimerosal-laden vaccines in 2002.

Prior to Modernization Act, however, neonates, infants, and children were subjected to toxic amounts of mercury via thimerosal in their vaccines. The Environmental Protection Agency posits that the safe limit for mercury exposure is .1 micrograms per kilogram per day, but vaccination schedules for children, starting in 1947, exceeded the EPA's safety limits for mercury exposure.

In 1947, the CDC recommended that children receive 13 vaccinations between the ages of two months and six months. One vaccination was for smallpox and four of the vaccinations were for diphtheria, pertussis (whooping cough) and tetanus. The latter three vaccinations were combined in one formulation – the "DTP" vaccine – and children between the ages of two and six months would receive four DTP vaccines. The smallpox vaccine didn't contain thimerosal, but each DTP vaccine contained about 25 micrograms of ethylmercury. The average weight of a two-month infant is approximately 11 pounds or five kilograms, so two year olds were subjected to a fivefold greater volume of ethylmercury than the EPA asserts is safe for adults when receiving DTP vaccines.

Johnson and Johnson's RhoGAM vaccine was licensed in 1968 and introduced into the vaccination schedule for pregnant women with Rh-negative blood. Women who have Rh-negative blood are at risk of having a baby with a potentially dangerous form of anemia called Rh disease. In the United States, about 15 percent of the white population, 5 to 8 percent of the African-American and Hispanic populations, and 1 to 2 percent of the Asian and Native American populations are Rh-negative.

The RhoGAM vaccine was scheduled to be administered twice during pregnancy or at 28 weeks of gestation and once to an infant within 72 hours after birth. A single dose of RhoGAM contained about 10.5 micrograms of ethylmercury, and thus, the RhoGAM vaccine subjected neonates and newborns to deleterious levels of ethylmercury. Bayer's BayRHo-D was licensed in 1971 for pregnant women with Rh-negative blood. BayRHo-D contains about 35 micrograms of ethyl mercury, and it too was administered to pregnant women. Shortly after RhoGAM and BayRHo-D vaccines were introduced into vaccination schedules, the rates of autism started to rise.

In 1981, the hepatitis B vaccine (HBV) became FDA approved. The recommended schedule for the HBV vaccine was at birth, two months, four months, and six months of age. Each of the HBV vaccines contained 12.5 micrograms of ethylmercury.

The *Haemophilus influenzae* type b (Hib) vaccine, which prevents meningitis, pneumonia, and other infections related to *Haemophilus influenzae* type b, was licensed in 1985. The Hib vaccine was initially administered at two months, and it was then administered on two additional occasions before the age of six months. A booster of the Hib vaccine was also administered at between 12 and 15 months. Each of the Hib vaccines contained about 25 micrograms of ethylmercury.

Consequently, throughout the 1980s and 1990s, even if American children didn't receive the RhoGAM or BayRHo-D vaccinations, they were injected with 237.5 micrograms of ethylmercury via the DTP, Hib, and HBV vaccines by the age of six months and that's excluding a flu vaccination at 6 months. The average flu vaccine contains about 25 micrograms of ethylmercury, so millions of American children were administered over 250 micrograms of ethylmercury subcutaneously by the age of six months.

25

As previously mentioned, mercury has been linked to autism, and the growth of autism in the U.S. starts to markedly proliferate as American children start receiving additional vaccines laden with mercury in the 1980s.

CHAPTER FIVE

THE FLU SHOT

As my odyssey to understand autism and vaccinations progressed, I visited numerous websites that both supported and opposed viewpoints with regards to vaccinations manufacturing autism. As I started to amass considerable evidence that vaccines played an integral role in the autism epidemic, I struggled to understand why the government, specifically the CDC, had been asleep at the wheel regarding the revelations I was starting to encounter.

I eventually found one website, Vaccine Liberation Army (VLA), that would eventually have a seismic impact on my understanding of government malfeasance regarding vaccines. The website featured a number of stories about the potential lethal toxicity of the influenza vaccine, and how powerful interests in the government and the pharmaceutical industry spun facts into fictions and fictions into fact. Although this digression on the seemingly innocuous flu shot is a departure from autism, which is the crux of book, I've since come to believe that the influenza vaccine provides a superlative microcosm and, for that matter, a superlative vantage point to view the delirium that succors the brave new world of runaway vaccinations.

After I read a disturbing article on the VLA website that discussed how various states were forcing parents to vaccinate their children, I posted a comment. Two days later, I received an email response from Eileen Dannemann, who's the founder of the Vaccine Liberation Army and also the director of the National Coalition for Women.

Her email discussed a study conducted by Dr. Gary Goldman that cited a 4,250 percent increase in the number of miscarriages and stillbirths reported to VAERS during the 2009/2010 flu season. The study also pointed out an astonishing fact: *The CDC had recommended the double-dosing of pregnant women with the H1N1 influenza vaccine. Although vaccines containing thimerosal began to be phased out in 1999, the flu shot had been exempt from that ruling, so the H1N1 vaccine contained thimerosal.*

Dr. Goldman's study was finally published in the May 2013 issue of the *Human and Environmental Toxicology Journal*.[1] In addition to Dr. Goldman's study demonstrating a 4,250 percent spike in miscarriages and stillbirths, he also showed that the CDC manipulated the data associated with the number of fetal deaths between 2009 and 2010.

Despite the smoking gun evidence unearthed by Dr. Goldman, Dr. Marie McCormick, chairperson of the CDC's H1N1 Vaccine Safety Risk and Assessment Working Group, knowingly submitted misleading documentation that denied evidence of adverse outcomes in pregnant women during the 2009-2010 N1H1 flu campaign to the Department of Health and Human Services. The CDC also failed to notify doctors about the risks of the flu shot, and they continued to double-dose their pregnant patients with harmful flu shots that collectively delivered up to 50 micrograms of ethylmercury. Due to the CDC's willful cover up, pregnant women are now pressured to get two flu vaccinations and two DTP vaccinations.

The CDC's party-line is that the risk of injury from the flu vaccine is greatly outweighed by the risk of contracting influenza, but there are at least 66 possible adverse reactions listed in CDC's literature that are associated with the influenza vaccine. The adverse reactions include anaphylactic shock, encephalopathy, neuropathic pain, seizures, and Guillian-Bare Syndrome (GBS), which is a painful autoimmune disorder that can lead to paralysis.

Unfortunately, most people who receive the flu shot have no idea that one possible side effect of the flu shot is

1   Goldman GS. Comparison of VAERS fetal-loss reports during three consecutive influenza seasons: was there a synergistic fetal toxicity associated with the two-vaccine 2009/2010 season.Hum ExpToxicology. 2013 May; 32(5): 464-75. PMID 23023030. PMC 3888271.

GBS. The CDC claims between 3,000 and 6,000 Americans will acquire GBS every year whether or not they receive a flu shot. The CDC also claims that the increased risk of acquiring GBS as the result of getting the flu vaccine is negligible – less than 2 cases per million doses. However, between 1993 and 1994 twice the typical yearly rate of GBS was reported following influenza vaccinations. Most cases weren't that severe, but fatalities did occur. Although the CDC acknowledges that people have a greater risk of acquiring GBS after receiving a flu vaccine if GBS runs in their family, it maintains that the increased risk is only one additional case per million persons vaccinated.

Joan Beecher, a former nursing professor at Southern Connecticut University, takes no consolation in the CDC's assurances. She developed GBS four weeks after receiving a seasonal flu shot. By all standards, Joan was the picture of health before the flu shot, but within two months, she was paralyzed and in omnipresent pain. Her physicians conceded that it was the worst case of GBS they had ever encountered, and they also conceded that her flu shot was the cause. Joan spent 18 months in the hospital due to GBS, and at the time Joan was hospitalized there were seven known vaccine-induced GBS cases at the same hospital.

During the 2009 H1N1 campaign, 46 million Americans were vaccinated with thimerosal-laden flu shots. One CDC statistic shows that between 3,000 and 49,000 people die from the flu each year.[2] However, based on the CDC's National Vital Statistics System only 500 people died from the flu in 2010. The significantly higher claim of 49,000 includes deaths from the flu and pneumonia combined. Granted, pneumonia can certainly be a complication of the flu. However, pneumonia can be acquired in a number of different ways. According to the National Center for Health Statistics (NCHS), influenza claimed 62,034 lives in 2001, 61,777 deaths were attributed to pneumonia, 257 deaths to the flu, and only 18 deaths were positively identified as the flu virus. On average,

---

2   www.cdc.gov/flu/about/diease/US_flu-related_deaths.htm.

only 1348 deaths have been attributed to the flu annually between 1979 and 2001.[3]

The CDC admits that they do not know exactly how many people die from seasonal flu each year. Influenza does not cause most pneumonia and influenza deaths. The CDC estimates that only 8.5 percent of all pneumonia and influenza deaths, and 2.1 percent of all respiratory and circulatory deaths were influenza related.[4] Moreover, in 2013, the CDC publicly confessed that the flu vaccine was only nine percent effective among patients over 65 years of age. On the whole, flu vaccinations produce negligible results.

A study conducted by researchers in eight European countries reported that vaccine effectiveness against influenza was only 38 percent effective in the beginning of the flu season, and its effectiveness diminished to less than one percent over a relatively short period of time.[5] Since the CDC began keeping track in 2004, overall vaccine effectiveness (VE) of the flu shot has been between 10 percent and 60 percent effective.[6] In January of 2015, the CDC claimed the flu shot to only be 23 percent effective.

Despite flu shots lack of efficacy and their potentially fatal adverse events, the vaccines seem to be ubiquitous, because now they're even administered by pharmacies. Pharmacies account for a significant number of flu vaccinations annually. For example, Walgreens alone administered 5.5 million flu shots in 2012, which generated approximately $82 million in additional profits that year for the retail drug store chain.

On January 13, 2013 New York Governor Andrew Cuomo declared an executive order that suspended the law prohibiting pharmacists from giving flu shots to children under 18 years of age! He said it was necessary, and declared a state

3   Doshi P. Are US flu deaths more PR than science. BMJ 2005 Dec 10; 331: 1412.
4   www.cdc.gov/flu/about/disease/US_Flu_related_deaths.htm.
5   January 2013, the CIDRAP news (Center for Infectious Disease and Research Policy). Vaccine Efficacy against A/H3H2 influenza virus.
6   Michael T Osterholm; et al. Efficacy and effectiveness of influenza vaccines: a systematic review and meta-analysis. The Lancet. 2012 Jan; 12(1): 36-44. No published meta-analyses have addressed efficacy and effectiveness of licensed influenza vaccines in the USA with highly specific diagnostic tests to confirm influenza.

of "health emergency" due to a flu outbreak. He publicly urged parents to have all their children – ages six months to 18 months – vaccinated for the flu. Fortunately, his executive order was only to remain in effect for 30 days. New York State had previously mandated that a pharmacist couldn't administer drugs or medication without a prescription, but during the 2013, declared state of emergency, they could give flu shots en masse.

Despite the questionable efficacy of flu vaccinations, and their potential to induce serious adverse events, the current market is flooded with flu vaccines. With the exception of Medimune's FluMist, which is sprayed into the nose, the balance of the flu shots marketed in the U.S. are administered subcutaneously. The following injectable flu vaccines that are currently marketed in the U.S. contain thimerosal:

- Fluzone (Sanofi Pasture)
- Fluvirin (Novartis)
- Afluria (Merck)
- FluLaval (Biomedical Corporation)

The following injectable flu vaccines that are currently marketed in the U.S. contain no thimerosal:

- Afluria (Merck)
- Fluzone (Sanofi Pasture)
- Fluzone High Dose (Sanofi Pasture)
- Fluzone intradermal (Sanofi Pasture)
- Agriflu (Novartis)
- Fluarix (GlaxoSmithKline)
- Flucelvax (Novartis)
- Flublok (Protein Sciences Corporation)
- Panblock (Protein Sciences Corporation)
- FluNhance (Protein Sciences Corporation)

Afluvira, Fluzone, Fluvirin, and Flulaval are trivalent vaccines, which means that they provide immunity against three active flu strains: one influenza type A subtype H1N1 virus strain, one influenza type A subtype H3N2 virus strain, and one influenza type B virus strain. Fluzone and Fluarix are quadrivalent vaccines, providing immunization against one influenza type A subtype H1N1 virus strain, one influenza type A subtype H3N2 virus strain, and two influenza type B virus strains.

Although vaccines have the possibility to produce adverse events, Sanofi-Pasture's Fluzone has been shown to be potentially lethal. During the 2013-2014 flu season, Sanofi-Pasture offered its high-dose Fluzone vaccine to seniors 65 years of age and older. A CVS promotional website assured seniors that receiving a high-dose Fluzone vaccine is harmless, and that the vast majority of the people in clinical studies who received Fluzone had minimal to no side effects. But even Sanofi-Pasture confessed that 6% of Fluzone recipients died after receiving the two types of Fluzone during clinical trials.[7] Within six months post vaccination, 156 Fluzone high-dose recipients, and 93 Fluzone recipients experienced a serious adverse event. No deaths were reported within 28 days post vaccination. But a total of 23 deaths were reported during the period 29 to 181 days post vaccination, 16 among high-dose Fluzone recipients, and 7 among standard dose Fluzone recipients.

Sanofi manufactures both thimerosal containing and non-thimerosal containing formulations of Fluzone, but both vaccines have the same name. So a reader of this book who decides to be vaccinated with Fluzone, but nonetheless wishes to avoid thimerosal should proceed with caution. In 2013, the Cayuga County Health Department of New York offered thimerosal free flu vaccines, but when its thimerosal free stock became depleted, the only available influenza vaccine offered, even to pregnant women, was thimerosal-laden.

The vast majority of flu vaccines are grown in fertilized chicken eggs using a 60-year-old method that requires hun-

7   reference: www.fda.gov/downloads/BiologicsBloodvaccines/Vaccines/ApprovedProducts/UCM305079.pdf.

dreds of millions of eggs. The technique can take up to six months to produce a vaccine, and it's prone to manufacturing problems. After experts at the World Health Organization and the FDA predict the flu strains that will be triggering most of the influenza in the upcoming season, strains of the flu are extracted from people who are infected, and then they're grown in live chicken eggs. At every step there is risk for contamination, and some flu strains are very difficult to cultivate in eggs.

In 2006, the government's quest to seemingly vaccinate every American for the flu was stepped up, and the Department of Health and Human Services allocated more than $1 billion in contracts to six U.S. manufacturers to develop new flu vaccine technology in the United States. In 2009, Health and Human Services provided Novartis with nearly $500 million to construct a U.S. facility capable of producing animal cell-based vaccines for seasonal and pandemic flu in the United States. Novartis picked up the rest of the estimated $1 billion price tag. In 2012, Novartis' Flucelvax, which is made from dog kidneys, was approved by the FDA.

The government also allocated Protein Sciences Corporation, which manufactures three vaccines, hefty grants. Protein Sciences Corporation was on the brink of economic extinction in 2009, but the U.S. government apparently believed in the company's good works and bailed it out. Protein Sciences Corporation secured an initial $35 million grant from the Department of Health and Human Services, and later it received a $147 million grant from the Biomedical Advanced Research and Development Authority, a branch of the Department of Health and Human Services, which provides "an integrated, systematic approach to the development and purchase of the necessary vaccines . . . "

Protein Sciences Corporation's FluBlok is made from a genetically modified baculovirus that is harvested from insect cells. It's indeed strange but true that the U.S. government pumped millions into a company that has created a flu vaccine derived from insects. It's perplexing that the government would be so keen on funding the development of FluBlok, because the FDA had rejected it on two previous occasions. Although FluBlok is devoid of thimerosal, aluminum, formaldehyde, and aborted fetal cell lines, the FDA obviously had reservations about the vaccine given its two prior FDA rejections, but Flublok was given the FDA seal of approval in 2013. The ostensible rationale offered by the government for its interest in FluBlok is that is can be produced much more expeditiously than traditional chicken embryo-based flu vaccines. The manufacturing process of FluBlok can be measured in weeks as opposed to months for traditional vaccines.

Despite Protein Sciences Corporation ostensibly working out the bugs of FluBlok, PSC conducted five clinical studies, consisting of approximately 4,400 FluBlok subjects. Some discovered that FluBlok wasn't innocuous. 122 Serious adverse events (SAE), and three deaths were reported. Three deaths out of 4,400 people may not seem like a lot, but the CDC's goal is to administer millions of these flu vaccinations. FluBlok is approved for use in persons 18 years of age and older. Protein Sciences Corporation forecasted that no less than 250,000 FluBlok vaccines would be available for the 2013-2014 flu season.[8] So the movie *Beetlejuice* now has a sequel that will be subcutaneously experienced by thousands of unwary Americans.

There are a plethora of new flu vaccines on the horizon, and Flublok was just a beginning to the innovativeness of flu vaccine manufacturers. Tobacco-based vaccines are currently in FDA trials. But my personal favorite is the lettuce-based vaccines. However, with millions of dollars currently in place for tobacco-based vaccine funding, lettuce-based vaccines will make a belated entry into the market.

Insect-based vaccines, tobacco-based vaccines, and lettuce-based vaccines sound like a Brave New World, but the profits to be derived from flu vaccines shine a light on the frenzied innovation behind Big Pharma's quest to produce novel vaccines. The research group Datamonitor Healthcare estimates that Big Pharma reaped approximately $3.7

8   Resource: Protein Sciences Corporation Influenza Vaccine Package Insert BLA STN 125285. www.fda.gov/downloads/BiologicalBloodVaccines/Vaccines/ApprovedProducts/UCM336020.pdf.

billion in 2012 from flu vaccines. Sanofi-Pasture's cut of that lucrative pie was $1.2 billion, and the vast majority of those profits were derived from its potentially lethal Fluzone. Given the colossal profits to be made from flu vaccines, flu vaccines' lack of efficacy and potential to produce adverse events, including death, will seemingly not be a hindrance as new flu vaccines are introduced to the American public. At this point in the story, the reader may start to think that the vaccine industry might sound a little crazy, but the vaccine business is big business, netting over $25 billion a year, and $25 billion can buy a lot of clout.

CHAPTER SIX

THE GOVERNMENT AND BIG PHARMA: A LOVE STORY

T he partnership between the government and Big Pharma that allows deleterious vaccines to be dispensed to millions of Americans is a long and winding road. The Prescription Drug User Fee Act (PDUFA), signed into law by President George H.W. Bush in 1992, set up Americans for a disturbing relationship between their government and Big Pharma. The Prescription Drug User Fee Act extracts fees from Big Pharma that are paid directly to the FDA, so it can avoid standard FDA rules and regulations when ushering new drugs to market. Since the formation of the FDA in 1906, and prior to 1992, the US Treasury solely funded it.

The FDA Commissioner under Bush I, Dr. David Kessler, assured Congress that the fees extracted from Big Pharma would enable the FDA to cut the approval time of new drugs in half. Before the Act was signed into law, it could take the FDA years to review new medications. But after Prescription Drug User Fee Act, the FDA's decisions on "break through" drugs could usher those drugs to market in just six months.

The Prescription Drug User Fee Act (PDUFA) was renewed in 1997 (PDUFA II), 2002 (PDUFA III), 2007 (PDUFA IV), and on July 9th, 2012, President Obama kept the ball rolling, reauthorizing the fifth version of PDUFA for another five years. In theory this law was supposed to give patients access to new, safe, and effective medicines ... in theory.

The FDA's "Accelerated Approval and Priority Review Program" was established in 1992 to accommodate the Prescription Drug User Fee Act. The Accelerated Approval and Priority Review Program allowed for the approval of drugs for serious or life-threatening diseases, based on their clinical benefit in Phase II trials. Thereby, streamlining the process for Big Pharma to usher drugs to market, because Big Pharma would be permitted to bypass costly and protracted Phase III clinical trials. Phase III clinical trials can comprise the majority of the developmental costs associated with ushering a drug to market. The issues that arise when drugs are in clinical trials include unexpected safety issues or failure to demonstrate efficacy. (*Forbes* reported that 95% of the experimental medications that are studied in humans fail to be either safe or effective).

The Prescription Drug User Fee Act and Accelerated Approval and Priority Review Program have created a cozy relationship between the FDA and Big Pharma at our expense. When we place our trust in a government agency that's receiving funds from an industry it's regulating, a salient conflict of interest occurs. Consequently, Americans now have an understaffed FDA that is ill equipped to ensure the safety and welfare of FDA approved medicines, and, since 1992, it is clearly under additional pressure not to bite the hand that feeds them.

The end result of PDUFA is that drugs have the potential to be approved too quickly – drugs that should not have been approved in the first place. In 2014, the PDUFA application fee for a new drug was $2,169,100 per application requiring clinical data, and half that amount for applications not-requiring clinical data. This would give the FDA all the grease it needed to keep rolling, and approximately 2,169,100 reasons to "fast-track" anything that crossed over its desk.

The FDA has 33 advisory committees, which are the most transparent function of the FDA approval process. Committees meet in public to review controversial medical products, and examine applications for FDA approval. Committee members are chosen experts in their respective fields, who are supposed to provide objective and diverse perspectives. This too sounds good in theory.

The problem is that the FDA frequently ends up approving products that the Advisory Committees vote against, because committees are under a great deal of pressure to recommend approvals. Often times, their votes for approval do not reflect the true committee's concerns about safety and efficacy.

Even when a majority of advisory committees do not recommend products, the FDA can give them a "green light." Another problem with these committees is conflicts of interest, because FDA panel members who have associations with drug manufactures, whose drugs they want approved, should recuse themselves. Instead, the FDA grants "waivers" for committee members who have obvious conflicts of interest.

In truth, the cronyism between the FDA and Big Pharma has allowed several drugs over the years to be FDA approved, even though the drugs have proven to be harmful and even fatal. One example of the FDA abrogating its due diligence is GlaxoSmithKline's Avandia.

GlaxoSmithKline (GSK) is one of the world's largest pharmaceutical companies, with total annual revenues approaching $46 billion. GSK manufactures vaccines and other prescription drugs for a variety of medical conditions that are approved by the FDA. In 1999, GlaxoSmithKline introduced the anti-diabetic drug Avandia to the market. It had long been suspected that Avandia had an unfavorable safety profile prior to its FDA approval, and by 2007 it was either suspected or held responsible in over 100,000 deaths and heart attacks. The European Union's European Medicines Agency, which is America's equivalent to the FDA, recommended an immediate recall of Avandia.

In 2010, the FDA finally decided to admonish GSK for Avandia. The FDA didn't recall Avandia, but rather slapped GSK on the wrist by mandating that Avandia be accompanied by a Risk Evaluation and Mitigation Strategy or REMS warning. Despite the REMS warning accompanying Avandia, it was still available to Americans provided they were aware of its risks. In 2010, GSK had paid over $500 million in lawsuit settlements due to Avandia.

In 2012, GSK also pleaded guilty to criminal charges, and agreed to pay $3 billion in fines for promoting the unapproved use of drugs and failing to report safety data. Avandia would be one of the drugs that the Department of Justice concluded GSK had failed to be less than forthcoming about its safety data.

But in a miraculous turnaround in June 2013, the FDA voted to allow Avandia to be marketed in the US without a REMS warning. The FDA's Joint Advisory Committee determined that Avandia was safe again, despite the fines and lawsuits. The Joint Advisory Committee based its decision on an independent study conducted by Duke University's Clinical Research Institute. Shortly before Duke University found Avandia to be "safe," GSK awarded Duke $1.65 million dollars to conduct clinical health studies.

But, alas, Avandia, the malfeasance of GSK, and the seeming schizophrenia of the FDA are not isolated instances of a perfidious medical industrial complex that is rife with corruption and allows lethal drugs to be introduced to the American public. The rise and fall of Vioxx and the malfeasance of New Jersey-based pharmaceutical and vaccine manufacturer Merck is quite a disturbing tale.

Merck's Vioxx, a non-steroidal, anti-inflammatory drug (NSAID) for the treatment of pain, received FDA approval in May of 1999 and Merck withdrew it from the market in September of 2004. Unfortunately, Vioxx left a huge wake of carnage and death in the years that Merck aggressively marketed the drug. Indeed, it's been described as the worst drug disaster in history, because of the thousands of Americans who had fatal heart attacks due to the drug.

The suspicions that Merck and the FDA teamed up to make Vioxx a blockbuster drug run deep. Early in the development of Vioxx, Merck attempted to convince the FDA that Vioxx was better than other NSAIDs, because it caused fewer digestive tract problems. Even before the drug was FDA approved in 1999, the company launched its Vioxx Gastrointestinal Outcomes Research study (VIGOR) to assess Vioxx's digestive risks.

The VIGOR study showed that Vioxx was easier on the digestive system than other NSAIDs, but it also demonstrated that Vioxx increased the risk of heart problems. The VIGOR study was published in the prestigious *New England Journal of Medicine*, but the VIGOR researchers neglected to include the extent of the heart and stroke problems that were produced by Vioxx.[1]

After the VIGOR study, Merck continually hounded the FDA to allow the drug to drop the digestive warnings on the label. In February 2001, the FDA acquiesced to Merck's request to change the drug's label to reflect that it's safer on the stomach than other NSAIDs. Although the FDA was aware of Vioxx's potential to induce heart and stroke problems, the FDA didn't require Merck to include the enhanced risk of strokes and heart attacks on its label until April 2002, years after the VIGOR trial results showed the risks. Critics of the Vioxx debacle would later point to this as evidence of the cozy relationship between Merck and the FDA that generated the FDA's blasé attitude towards Vioxx's health risks.

Finally, in 2004, David Graham, MD, MPH, the associate director for science and medicine at the FDA's Office of Drug Safety, which is responsible for monitoring the safety of drugs already on the market, oversaw an analysis on a database of 1.4 million Kaiser Permanente members.[2] The analysis conducted by Graham and his colleagues conclud-

---

1   Bombardier C., M.D.: et al. Comparison of upper gastrointestinal toxicity of Robecoxib and Naproxen in patients with rheumatoid arthritis VIGOR Study Group. N Eng J Med. 2000 Nov 23; 343(21): 1520-8. PMID: 11087881.
2   Mark Greener, First do no harm. Improving drug safety through legislation and Independent research. EMBO Rep 2008 March; 9(3) 221-224 PMCID:P-MC 2267386.

ed that Vioxx was responsible for 38,000 heart attacks and sudden cardiac deaths. Graham would later tell a US Senate subcommittee that 38,000 heart attacks and sudden cardiac deaths was a conservative estimate. He felt that Vioxx was probably responsible for between 88,000 and 139,000 heart attacks and subsequently 26,000 to 41,000 deaths.

Before the Senate subcommittee, Dr. Graham testified that when his team concluded its study and prepared to present its results, it was attacked by various sectors of the FDA, and he feared the loss of his job.[3] "I was pressured to change my conclusions and recommendations, and basically threatened that if I did not change them, I would not be permitted to present" the paper reporting his study's conclusions. Despite the heat that was applied to Dr. Graham, he persevered with the publication of his study, and Merck withdrew Vioxx from the market shortly before Dr. Graham's results were published.

In a 2005 interview, Dr. Graham said, "The FDA is inherently biased in favor of the pharmaceutical industry. It views industry as its client, whose interests it must represent and advance. It views its primary mission as approving as many drugs it can, regardless of whether the drugs are safe or needed."

Although Merck essentially lied about the lethality of Vioxx by withholding data that was generated from the VIGOR study, and subsequently caused the death of thousands of Americans, it was merely fined and charged with the misdemeanor.

The cronyism between the government and Big Pharma is alive and well for vaccines too. Although vaccines are subject to the same FDA approval process as prescription drugs, the government actually protects vaccine manufacturers from civil lawsuits when their vaccines trigger harmful and injurious after effects.

In the 1970's and 1980's, many Americans became much less concerned about the prevention of infectious diseases,

---

3   US Senate (2004) Testimony of David J. Graham, M.D., MPH November 18, 2004. www.finance.senate.gov/imo/media/doc/111804dgtest.pfd.

and their concerns shifted to risk of injury from the vaccines themselves. A contingent of parents specifically blamed the diphtheria, tetanus, and pertussis (DTP) vaccine for injuring their children, which resulted in a sharp increase in vaccine related lawsuits. Between 1978 and 1981, only nine product liability suits were filed against DTP manufacturers. By the mid-80's, the lawsuits against the manufacturers of the DTP vaccine numbered over 200 a year. The lawsuits crippled the DTP vaccine market. Two out of the three domestic manufacturers of the DTP vaccine withdrew their vaccines. The remaining manufacturer, Lederal Laboratories, estimated its potential liability significantly exceeded its annual sales, because Lederal was crippled by the litigation, and DTP vaccine shortages arose in 1984.

The litigants found it very costly and difficult to pursue lawsuits against the vaccine manufacturers, and many parents started to refuse to have their children vaccinated. To counteract the downward trend in vaccinations, the government enacted the National Childhood Vaccine Injury (NCVI) Act in 1986. NCVI acknowledged that vaccine injuries and deaths are real and that the vaccine injured and their families should be financially supported and that vaccine safety protections were needed in the mass vaccination system, but the law didn't mention autism. The law also exempted Big Pharma from being sued when its vaccines caused injuries. The following is an excerpt from Section 22(b)(1) of the NCVI:

> No vaccine manufacturer shall be liable in a civil action for damages arising from a vaccine-related injury or death associated with the administration of a vaccine after October 1, 1988, if the injury or death resulted from side effects that were unavoidable even though the vaccine was properly prepared and was accompanied by proper directions and warnings.

The National Vaccine Injury Compensation Program (VICP) was created under the National Childhood Vaccine Injury Act to institute a no-fault, non-adversarial alternative to suing vaccine manufacturers and providers in civil court. The VICP is a no fault tort system for resolving vaccine injury claims, and it provides compensation to those people found to be injured by vaccines.

After the VICP was created, the government decreed that no vaccine manufacturer would be liable in a civil action for damages arising from an injury or death associated with the administration of a vaccine after October 1st, 1988.

Instead of suing vaccine manufacturers, the VICP fund compensates vaccine related injuries or death for specified vaccines.

To subsidize the VICP fund, the CDC levies an excise tax of 75¢ on each vaccine that theoretically prevents a respective disease. For example, a single influenza vaccine is levied 75¢, and a multi-dose vaccine such as the Measles, Mumps, Rubella (MMR) vaccine is taxed $2.25, because it theoretically prevents three diseases.

Since the initial VICP claims were made in 1989, a total of $2.27 billion in payments have been made to 2,900 petitioners, but, as of April 2012, 8,700 cases have been dismissed. Seeking compensation from the VICP is extremely difficult and arduous, especially for autism, because the vast majority of "scientific" studies haven't found a discernable link between vaccines and autism.

The Homeland Security Act, established November 25th, 2002 in the wake of the September 11th, 2001 terrorist attacks by President George W. Bush, further reinforced the VICP. According to the Homeland Security Act, pharmaceutical companies can escape liability lawsuits, via the Homeland Security Department, by invoking the red herring that such litigation infringes on national security.

Thus, the Homeland Security Act gives pharmaceutical companies further immunity from vaccine injuries and fatalities even if the manufacturer is willfully negligent, even though liability lawsuits against vaccine manufacturers have absolutely no connection to the "War on Terror." A provision of the bill gives pharmaceutical companies an exemption from FOIA too. Interestingly, President Bush II named Sidney Taurel, CEO for Eli Lilly, to the Homeland Security Advisory Counsel. President Bush's father, H.W. also sat on Eli's board in the 70's.

After the passage of the Homeland Security Act, three government agencies currently play a roll in the VICP: The US Department of Health and Human Services (HHS), the US Department of Justice (DOJ), and the US Court of Federal Claims. The Office of Special Masters is an adjunct. The US Court of Federal Claims is the ultimate arbitrator of vaccine injury claims.

In July of 2002, the Office of Special Masters issued Autism General Order #1, which established the protocols for addressing the thousands of vaccine injury claims that it anticipated. Autism General Order #1 created the Omnibus Autism Proceeding that assigned three special masters to adjudicate the flood of autism lawsuits. Special masters are frequently, but not necessarily attorneys, who supervise the protocols of the Office of Special Masters court to ensure that court protocols are being followed.

As of August 2010, over 5,600 vaccine injury cases have been filed with the Office of Special Masters, and over 5,000 cases were pending. Because there are only three special masters overseeing thousands of cases, the process is very, very slow and tedious. For example, although the Omnibus Autism Proceeding was created in July of 2002, the Office of Special Masters adjudicated the first case of vaccine injury resulting in autism, initiated by the parents of 12-year-old Michelle Cedillo, in June of 2007. So it took five years for the Cedillo case to wend its way through the Office of Special Masters bureaucratic red tape.

Michelle Cedillo suffers from severe autism, inflammatory bowel disease, glaucoma, and epilepsy and she finally had her hearing before the Office of Special Masters On June 11th, 2007. Special Master George Hastings, Jr., pledged to listen carefully to the evidence presented during the Cedillo hearing. But after listening to the evidence, he referenced an extremely flawed 2004 Institute of Medicine report, which will be discussed in a subsequent chapter, that quelled the notion that there was any association between thimerosal and autism, and he ruled against Michelle Cedillo receiving compensation from the VICP.

As previously mentioned, because "scientific data" fails to support the link between vaccines and autism, successful plaintiffs before the Office of Special Masters generally have to demonstrate that the vaccine in question induced damage or malfunction of the brain, inflammation of the brain, seizures, etc.

The parents of Kenneth Banks appeared before the Office of Special Masters the following month. Their son, Bailey, received a measles, mumps, and rubella (MMR) vaccine vaccination on March 14th, 2002, during his 15th month checkup. At the time he received the MMR vaccine, he was a normal, healthy child, but he had a seizure 16 days after receiving an MMR vaccine. His mother noticed he was choking and his eyes were rolling backward. Bailey was rushed to the emergency room, where he vomited three times. The examining physician characterized his condition as a "new onset seizure." He was admitted to the hospital for observation. The next day Bailey was given an MRI scan of his brain, and the radiologist determined the scan was consistent with acute disseminated encephalomyelitis (ADEM), which usually occurs following a viral infection, and it involves autoimmune demyelination that is characteristic of multiple sclerosis. ADEM has been linked to the MMR vaccine in previous cases.[4]

April 10th, 2000, Bailey was given a full neurological exam. The examination revealed slight left "esotropia" (inward turning of one or both eyes), and his gait was extremely impaired. The examining neurologist concluded he suffered from a gross motor developmental delay and "strabismus," which involves the eyes pointing in different directions. Based on the MRI, he felt that Bailey's moderate "hypomyelination" was consistent with ADEM, but he didn't make a definitive diagnosis of ADEM. The neurolo-

---

4   http://myelitis.org/symptoms-conditions/acute-disseminated-encephalomyelitis/.

gist recommended further lab tests, an ophthalmology consultation, and a physical therapy evaluation.

January 5th, 2001, an MRI was performed Bailey that showed the same results as the prior MRI. Approximately three weeks after the latter MRI, Bailey was examined by another neurologist, who determined that he suffered from global developmental delays, including features associated with *pervasive developmental disorders* (*PDD*). The doctor noted some cognitive progress since Bailey's last neurological visit. Bailey was able to assist in dressing, and he drank from a cup, but he added that the child was severely developmentally delayed.

In June of 2007, Special Master Richard Abell ruled that Bailey, now age 10, should be awarded a lump sum of lump sum of $810,000, plus an estimated $30-40,000 per year for various services and care. Special Master Abell concluded that the evidence presented demonstrated that Bailey suffered from ADEM, and ADEM had been linked to the MMR vaccine in previous cases. The Special Master then determined from the testimony heard in court that ADEM could ultimately result in "Pervasive Developmental Delay – Not Otherwise Specified," commonly referred to as PDD-NOS, which is on the spectrum of autism disorders.

The Baileys and their legal counsel approached their hearing before the Office of Special Masters in a very intelligent and strategic manner. They avoided saying that the MMR vaccine that Bailey received resulted in his autism, but, rather, they argued that the MMR vaccine caused ADEM, which resulted in PDD-NOS. If they had simply told the truth, which was that the MMR vaccine was responsible for Bailey's autism, then they would've had the same outcome as Michelle Cedillo and her parents.

Every parent should carefully document their child's condition and/or adverse reactions following a vaccination. Immediate and proper medical intervention could potentially have enormous benefits down the road if your child is the victim of a vaccine injury. Parents who suspect their child is the victim of a vaccine injury can visit the U.S. Court of Federal Claims website to obtain valuable information on how to file a claim to opinions and decisions on current cases. The web address is www.uscfc.uscourts.gov/opinions_decisions_vaccine/unpublished.

The case of Hannah Bruesewitz was brought before the Court of Special Masters on December 20, 2002. Hannah's case would not only exemplify the callous disregard of the Court of Special Masters Court, but also the government's vehement protection of Big Pharma, when its vaccines cause irreversible injuries and grievous harm.

Hannah Bruesewitz was a healthy five-month-old infant when she received a thimerosal laden DTP vaccine that was manufactured by Lederal Laboratories in 1992. Shortly after receiving the DTP vaccine, Hannah began experiencing seizures. Over the next month, Hannah experienced more than 100 seizures, and she was eventually diagnosed with "residual seizure disorder" and "developmental delay."

In April 1995, Hannah's parents, Russ and Robalee Bruesewitz, filed a petition in the VICP. Finally, on December 20, 2002, seven years after the petition was filed, a special master categorically rejected her claim, which hardly complies with Congress' promise in the 1986 NCVI that awards be "made to vaccine-injured persons quickly, easily, and with certainty and generosity."

In October 2005, the Bruesewitzes filed a lawsuit in Pennsylvania state court alleging the defective design of the DTP vaccine Hannah received caused her injuries. In the interim, Wyeth had bought Lederal Laboratories, and Wyeth had the Bruesewitzes lawsuit moved to federal court, where the District Court for the Eastern District of Pennsylvania dismissed the Bruesewitzes' lawsuit, citing the NCVI.

In March 2009, the US Third Circuit Court affirmed the decision of the District Court for the Eastern District of Pennsylvania, citing the NCVI. As Hannah's case was wending through the US courts, Pfizer, the world's largest pharmaceutical company, bought Wyeth. Pfizer then *encouraged* the Supreme Court to hear the Bruesewitz case to address potential similar claims in the future, because, Pfizer sought to end the issue once and for all.

The Supreme Court acquiesced to Pfizer, and agreed to hear the case of Bruesewitz vs. Wyeth. On February 21, 2011, the Supreme Court voted six to two to deny Hannah any compensation, essentially shielding Big Pharma from being sued by parents whose children were inured by its vaccines.

Justice Antonin Scalia wrote the majority opinion in which he stated that the NCVI "expressly exempted" Pfizer from being sued by the Bruesewitzes. Scalia also wrote that the Supreme Court agreed with Congress in the respect that side effects were "unavoidable" when a vaccine is given to millions of children. If the drug makers could be sued and forced to pay huge claims for devastating injuries, the vaccine industry could be wiped out.

Despite the heartbreaking circumstances surrounding the case of Hannah Bruesewitz and the thousands of other children who have been irreversibly damaged by vaccines, the case of Bruesewitz vs. Wyeth demonstrates that the love affair between the government and Big Pharma is alive and well, regardless of the unnecessary and permanent injuries that are suffered by children who receive vaccines.

And that ominous love affair is further exemplified by the revolving door between the government and Big Pharma. A myriad of government officials who have pledged to serve and protect American citizens from the taint and corruption of Big Pharma have abrogated their responsibilities and seamlessly segued into prestigious positions with Big Pharma. For example, as CDC Director, Julie Gerberding had been a champion of vaccines, and when she left the CDC, she was anointed the president of Big Pharma bellwether Merck, a major producer of vaccines. Moreover, former NIH Director Elias Zerhouni left his government position and now heads Big Pharma bellwether Sanofi, a major producer of vaccines. And so it goes...

CHAPTER SEVEN

CONGRESS DEMANDS ANSWERS

A s the autism rates in the U.S. continued to soar in the 1980s and 1990s, the controversy surrounding vaccines and whether or not they engendered autism started to achieve a critical mass. In 1997, as previously mentioned, Congress passed the Food and Drug Administration Modernization Act, which called for an FDA review of all mercury containing food and drugs, including a review of vaccines that contain thimerosal.

The review was completed in 1999, and the FDA recognized that some children "could" be exposed to a cumulative level of mercury over the first 6 months of life that exceed the EPA's federal guidelines. In July 1999, public-health officials announced that thimerosal would be phased out of vaccines. The CDC, American Academy of Pediatrics, and FDA insisted that the measure was *purely precautionary*. So the government never stated that thimerosal was toxic and potentially injurious, but, rather, its removal from vaccines purely precautionary.

As a consequence of the FDA Modernization Act, the FDA was required to commission the Institute of Medicine to assess the impact of mercury in vaccines. The Institute of Medicine's study began in late 1999 with an expected publication date in 2001. The FDA Modernization Act forced the CDC to preempt the Institute of Medicine, because it was well aware of the connection between thimerosal and autism, due to the information in its Vaccine Safety Data-link (VSD). The CDC established the VSD in 1990 to assess the adverse side effects of vaccines, and it conscripted four HMOs, including Kaiser Permanente, to provide the CDC with medical data on vaccination histories, health outcomes, and subject characteristics. The VSD database contains data compiled from surveillance on more than seven million Americans, including about 500,000 children from birth through age six years, which is 2% of the U.S. population in this demographic.

The CDC ultimately tasked one of its young epidemiologists by the name of Dr. Thomas Verstraeten to compare neurodevelopmental outcomes of children exposed to thimerosal using the CDC's VSD. Dr. Verstraeten was aware of the CDC's party line that there was no relationship between mercury and autism, but his initial results demonstrated a 7.6-fold increased risk of autism from exposure to thimerosal during infancy, which caused quite a quandary for the CDC.

Through a Freedom of Information Act request, concerned parents obtained the frenzied email corresponences among Dr. Verstraeten and his colleagues at the CDC. In fact, Dr. Verstraeten warned the CDC not to focus on disproving an "unpleasant theory," rather, through the use of their limited available data, minimize the prevalence of autism for children who have received mercury laden vaccines. The CDC's Acting Associate Director for Science and Public Health, National Center On Birth Defects And Developmental Disabilities, Dr. Coleen Boyle, sent an email to Dr. Frank Destsfano, project director of the VSD, suggesting that he manipulate the data by adding 18 month and two year olds to the dataset, because they're too young to have an ASD diagnosis, and they would dilute the prevalence of children suffering from autism who had been vaccinated.

In spite of Dr. Verstraeten's stellar scientific custom tailored made-to-order study, the data failed to refute the legitimate connection between thimerosal, vaccines, and autism. An exasperated Dr. Verstraeten continued to manipulate the data, but his various machinations were not producing the desired results. At one point, he sent an email to a CDC colleague, discussing his various manipulations, and the subject line read: "It just won't go away."

In June of 2000, approximately six months after Dr. Ver-straeten's analysis demonstrated a definite link between vaccines with mercury and autism, the CDC held a private meeting at the Simpsonwood Conference Center in Atlanta, GA. The Simpsonwood conference included representatives from the CDC, FDA, World Health Organization (WHO) and various representatives of vaccine manufacturers. The CDC was forced to share some rather unsavory revelations with its distinguished guests: Although Dr. Verstraeten had repeatedly manipulated the data, the cold hard truth was that the link between thimerosal, vaccinations, and autism could not be dismissed.

Dr. Vertsraeten told those in attendance that infants who are exposed to vaccines with thimerosal in their first two months of life are vulnerable to "an unspecified developmental delay." He also told the group that infants who are exposed to vaccines with thimerosal during their first three months of life are susceptible to "tics." He went on to state that infants exposed to vaccines with thimerosal in their first six months of life are vulnerable to "attention deficit disorder" and a broad range of "neurodevelopmental delays."

The audience was stunned, because the vast majority of them had actually embraced the government's propaganda. "...the number of dose related relationships [between mercury and autism] are linear and statistically significant, said Dr. William Weil of the American Academy of Pediatrics. "You can play with this all you want. They are linear. They are statistically significant."

But Dr. Robert Chen, who was the CDC's Chief of Vaccine Safety and Development, nonetheless promulgated the CDC's party line due to the importance of vaccines protecting the children from the scourge of childhood illnesses: "...the issue is that it is impossible, unethical to leave kids unimmunized, so you will never, ever resolve that issue [regarding the impact of mercury]."

Dr. John Clements of the World Health Organization was particularly stunned, because WHO administered vaccines to over 100 million children. "But there is now the point at which the research results have to be handled, and even if this committee decides that there is no association and that information gets out, the work has been done and through the freedom of information that will be taken by others and will be used in other ways beyond the control of this group," said Dr. Clements. "And I am very concerned about that as I suspect that it is already too late to do anything regardless of any professional body and what they say...My mandate as I sit here in this group is to make sure at the end of the day that 100,000,000 are immunized with DTP, Hepatitis B and if possible Hib, this year, next year and for many years to come, and that will have to be with thimerosal containing vaccines unless a miracle occurs and an alternative is found quickly and is tried and found to be safe."

Approximately one year after the Simpsonwood conference on July 16th, 2001, the Institute of Medicine held a meeting in Boston, where Dr. Verstraeten was slated to publicly announce the results of his study that utilized the VSD data. Before his presentation, Dr. Verstraeten proclaimed that he had accepted a job offer "just that morning" from GlaxoSmithKline. The pharmaceutical company was anointing Dr. Verstraeten as the Associate Director of Epidemiology in its Belgium Division of Biologics. Dr. Verstraeten had accepted a job with a vaccine manufacturer in his native Belgium – out of the reach of US authorities, including Congress.

After Dr. Verstraeten publicly announced his upward mobility, he discussed his VSD analysis. At this point, his VSD analysis was in its third incarnation regarding the association between vaccines with thimerosal and autism, so it showed a slight correlation between thimerosal and ASD, but a correlation that wasn't statistically significant. (The fourth incarnation of the Verstraeten analysis was published in Pediatrics in 2003, and, by that time, the CDC had figured out how to dilute the data to show that no correlation existed between thimerosal and autism.)

Although the CDC and Big Pharma were engaged in a cover-up of monumental proportions, regarding vaccines and autism, they were managing to hoodwink the vast majority of Americans and also the elected officials of the body politic. But a few members of Congress weren't imbibing the subterfuge of the CDC and Big Pharma, and U.S. Representative Dan Burton, a Republican from Indiana, was one of them.

Burton's grandson, Christian, was a normal, healthy infant until he received a series of vaccinations in his second year of life. Prior to the vaccinations, Christian was on par with other infants his age with regards to walking, talking, and making eye contact. Two days after Christian received nine vaccinations in one day, he underwent an abrupt metamorphosis. He no longer spoke, and he shunned eye contact. He started to cry endlessly and bang his head against the wall too. He also began to suffer from chronic diarrhea and severe bowel problems. He has since been diagnosed with autism.

So Representative Burton had seen the deleterious effects of vaccines firsthand, and he was determined to augur into the cover-up. Representative Burton was in the perfect position to investigate the matter, because he chaired the Committee on Oversight and Government Reform of the House of Representatives. The Committee on Oversight and Government Reform is a United States House of Representatives committee that has existed in varying forms the early 1800s. The Committee's government-wide oversight jurisdiction and expanded legislative authority make it one of the most influential and powerful committees in the House. The Committee serves as Congress' primary investigative and oversight committee, and is granted broad jurisdiction.

Between April of 2000 and May of 2004, Burton chaired the Committee on Oversight and Government Reform's nine hearings on vaccines and/or autism:

- Autism: Present Challenges, Future Needs – Why the Increased Rates? (2000)

- Mercury in Medicine – Are We Taking Unnecessary Risks? (2000)

- Autism – Why the Increased Rates? A One-Year Update (2001)

- The Autism Epidemic – Is the NIH and CDC Response Adequate? (2002)

- The Status of Research into Vaccine Safety and Autism (2002)

- Vaccines and the Autism Epidemic: Reviewing the Federal Government's Track Record and Charting a Course for the Future (2002)

- The Future Challenges of Autism: A Survey of the Ongoing Initiatives in the Federal Government to Address the Epidemic (2002)

- Autism Spectrum Disorders: An Update of Federal Government Initiatives and Revolutionary New Treatment of Neuro-Developmental Diseases (2003)

- Truth Revealed: New Scientific Discoveries Regarding Mercury in Medicine and Autism (2004)

After the initial two Committee on Oversight and Government Reform hearings on autism in 2000 – "Autism: Present Challenges, Future Needs – Why the Increased Rates?" and "Mercury in Medicine – Are We Taking Unnecessary Risks?" – Representative Burton sent a letter to the Department of Health and Human Services, requesting that the FDA recall all vaccines that contained thimerosal. "We all know and accept that mercury is a neurotoxin, and yet the FDA has failed to recall the 50 vaccines that contain thimerosal," Burton wrote. "Every day that mercury-containing vaccines remain on the market is another day HHS is putting 8,000 children at risk." But his appeal fell on deaf ears.

Although Congressman Burton was tenacious and unyielding it was nonetheless impossible for him to persuade CDC personnel testifying before the various Committee on Oversight and Government Reform's hearings on autism to cough up the truth. A prime example of CDC personnel perjuring themselves before Congress is the testimony of Coleen Boyle, PhD, the CDC's Acting Associate Director for Science and Public Health, National Center on Birth Defects and Developmental Disabilities, before the 2001 hearing entitled "Mercury in Medicine – Taking Unnecessary Risks." The following is an excerpt from Dr. Boyle's testimony before the Committee on Oversight and Government Reform approximately one year after she suggested that Dr. Destefano, project director of the VSD, manipulate the VSD data by adding one and two year olds to the dataset, because they were too young to have an ASD diagnosis:

> Some parents have expressed concerns about a potential link between autism and vaccines currently being used in the United States. Although the weight of scientific evidence does not support such a link, CDC is strongly committed to assuring vaccine safety. CDC is actively involved in detecting and investigating vaccine safety concerns and supporting a wide range of vaccine safety research to address safety questions. A critical part of our vaccine safety effort is the objective, scientific evaluation of safety concerns by independent experts.

Representative Burton was incredulous of Dr. Boyle and her government cohorts. And following that hearing, he wrote a letter to Donna Shalala, Secretary of Health and Human Services that said, "Our children are the future of this country. As a Government we have a responsibility to do everything within our power to protect them from harm, including ensuring that vaccines are safe and effective. Every day that mercury-containing vaccines remain on the market is another day HHS is putting 8,000 children at risk. Given that Thimerosal-free vaccines are available and the known risk of mercury toxicity, to leave thimerosal-containing vaccines on the market is unconscionable.

Representative Dave Weldon, a Republican from Florida, shared Congressman Burton's concerns. Although Weldon hadn't been personally affected by autism, he was a medical doctor, and he had noticed a proliferation of autism rates. When he started medical school in the 1970s, he had never met anyone with an autistic child, and he hadn't encountered a single case of autism throughout his rotations in medical school. By the 1990s, however, he started to hear about numerous accounts of autism, and he sought answers too.

Congressmen Burton and Weldon rightfully perceived autism to be assuming epidemic proportions, and they felt that the government wasn't addressing it with the same gravitas that it addressed other epidemics. For example, the government monies earmarked for autism in 2002 and 2003, respectively, were $56 million and $70 million. In the same years the respective government monies earmarked for diabetes and HIV were $781.3 million and $845 million and $2 billion and $2.77 billion. The CDC's spending for autism was almost 80 times less than that for AIDS, and the CDC's spending for autism was five times less than that of diabetes.

One the principle reasons that inspired Congressmen Burton and Welton to spearhead a Congressional investigation into autism was to ensure that research into autism was conducted in a timely manner. In 2002, autism was burgeoning at a very high rate with each successive year, so they doggedly wanted to find answers to the causes of the epidemic and also solutions.

In April of 2002, the House Committee on Government Reform held a hearing entitled "The Status of Research into Vaccine Safety and Autism." And Dan Burton gave an impassioned opening statement: "Giving more money to research is not the only answer though. Oversight is needed to make sure that research that is funded will sufficiently answer the questions regarding the epidemic, how to treat autism, and how to prevent the next ten years from seeing the statistic of 1 in 250 from becoming 1 in 25 children."

Dr. Colleen Boyle was called to testify before the April of 2002 hearing too. She was questioned about the Verstraeten study and the CDC's reluctance to share information in the VSD with external researchers. Dr. Boyle, however, smoke screened the congressional panel. She cited a strong obligation to maintain the confidentiality of the data within the VSD, but she reassured the hearing that progress was being made for independent researchers to gain access to the VSD.

Throughout the 2002 hearing, Representative Burton couldn't prevent himself from tirades against the government's elaborate machinations that thwarted an accurate appraisal of the autism epidemic and also compensation for victims of vaccine related injuries. As previously mentioned, the Homeland Security Bill further blocked parents with autistic children from compensation via a civil lawsuit against the pharmaceutical companies who manufacture vaccines.

Representative Burton was cognizant of the fact that parents of autistic children ultimately ended up selling their homes and expending their life savings to care for their children. At one point in the hearing, he expressed his utter frustration with the Vaccine Injury Compensation Program (VICP): "Parents all over this country are going through the same thing, and they have no recourse. The VICP fund has a three-year statute of limitations. If they don't know within a three-year period that their child has been affected by these vaccines they're out of luck. They have no place to go but the courts."

At the hearing, Karen Midthun, MD, Director of the FDA's Office of Vaccines Research and Review, which evaluates the safety and efficacy of vaccines in the U.S., was called to testify. The following exchange from an increasingly bellicose Representative Burton and a nebulous Dr. Midthun encapsulates the hearing.

> **Representative Burton**: "Are there still vaccines in doctors offices today that contain thimerosal that are being given to children?"
>
> **Dr. Midthun**: "I don't believe so no. As I mentioned all vaccines for the routine recommended childhood vaccine immunization series started, either have been manufactured thimerosal free, or markedly reduced amounts of thimerosal..."
>
> **Representative Burton**: "But they still have thimerosal in them?"

Dr. Midthun: "Yes, yes..."

Representative Burton: "Every study that's been done doctor, that you guy's have put forth as showing that there's no correlation between thimerosal and autism, doesn't say categorically, that thimerosal doesn't cause autism. They never say that! Can you tell me right now, positively, categorically, without any doubt whatsoever that mercury in vaccines does not cause autism?"

Dr. Midthun: "I think what I'd have to say is what the IOM [Institute of Medicine] concluded that the body of evidence neither allows to accept or reject that relationship."

Representative Burton: "I want you to give me a yes or a no. . . . Can you tell me without any doubt whatsoever that the mercury in vaccines does not cause neurological problems or autism?"

Dr. Midthun: "We can neither accept or reject a cause of relationship."

Representative Burton: "Then why hasn't the FDA, to be on the safe side, knowing that we're having one in 250 and in some cases 1:150 children becoming autistic. And there's a growing body of evidence that thimerosal and mercury is causing that. Why wouldn't you go down the cautious road? Instead of coming up with these additional studies that say, 'Well ... we're not sure.' We can't you say yeah or neigh.... There's been 1,500 plus articles written saying that there is a problem. We've got scientists from all over the world coming in here. You saw video demonstration from a Canadian tape showing the impact of a minute amount of mercury in brain cells. And you continue to say, "Well, we don't think that a very small amount of mercury." But you don't know! Because there's no study that you've put out that I've seen, not one, that says categorically, that mercury in vaccines does not cause neurological problems. You can't tell me that today. You've hedged all over that issue. And you guys just keep coming up here and making excuses, and I don't know why. Why not just get it out of there!"

The stoic expression on Dr. Midthun's face ultimately crumbled like a child being severely scolded. But, at least, Dr. Midthun was accurate when she said, "We can neither accept or reject a cause of relationship" between thimerosal and autism. Indeed, Verstraeten's preliminary study results proved the association between thimerosal and autism, but the CDC conveniently deposited his study in a black hole that has been inaccessible even to Congress.

As the CDC was covering up the Verstraeten study, it was funding the work of Poul Thorsen, a Danish psychiatrist. The story of the CDC and Dr. Thorsen is a strange story indeed. The profuse research of Dr. Thorsen is one of the pillars that the CDC has used to demonstrate that thimerosal-laden vaccines have absolutely no links to autism. The studies he's co-authored have been published in the most esteemed medical and scientific journals that include *American Journal Epidemiology*,[1] *Arch Pediatrics Journal of Adolescent Medicine*,[2] *Pediatrics*,[3] and the *New England Journal of Medicine*.[4]

Dr. Thorsen participated in a landmark study that was published in *Pediatrics* in 2003 – "Thimerosal and the Occurrence of Autism: Negative Ecological Evidence From Danish Population-Based Data."[5] The study found that Denmark experienced a twenty-fold increase in autism after it banned mercury-based preservatives in its vaccines in 1995. Thorsen and his colleagues concluded that mercury could therefore not be the culprit behind the autism epidemic in

1   Larsson H.J., et al. Risk factors for autism: perinatal factors, parental psychiatric history, and socioeconomic status. Am J Epidemiology. 2005 May 15; 161(10): 916-25. PMID: 15870155.
2   Atladóttir H.O, et al. Time trends in reported childhood neuropsychic disorders: a Danish cohort study. Arch Pediatr Adolesc Med. 2007 Feb; 161(2): 193-8. PMID: 17283306.
3   Atladóttir H.O., et al. Association of family history of autoimmune diseases and autism spectrum disorders. 2009 Aug; 124(2): 687-94. PMID 19581261.
4   Madsen K.M., et al. A population-based study of measles, mumps, and rubella vaccination in autism. N Engl J Med. 2002 Nov 7; 347(19): 1477-82. PMID: 12421889.
5   Madsen KM; et al. Thimerosal and the occurrence of autism; negative ecological evidence from Danish population-based data. Pediatrics 2003 Sep;112(3 pt 1):604-6. PMID12949291.

Denmark. The CDC loved that study, and it extensively promoted the study to demonstrate that vaccines play no role in autism.

Like many of the sinister machinations that the CDC devises to exonerate mercury from its culpability in autism, the 2003 *Pediatrics* study was quite fraudulent if one scratches below the surface. The authors of the study failed to disclose that the increase in Danish autism rates was the result of new mandates requiring, for the first time, that autism cases be reported on the national registry. This new law and the opening of a clinic in Copenhagen dedicated to autism treatment accounted for the sudden rise in reported autism cases instead of the removal of mercury from vaccines. The *New York Times* has also relied on this study as the basis for its public assurances that mercury is safe to inject into young children.

The CDC had found a kindred spirit in Dr. Thorsen, and it lavished him with millions of dollars for his research. The CDC's Diana Schendel, PhD, teamed up with Dr. Thorsen, and they became a veritable Fred Astaire and Ginger Roberts of research, publishing 37 articles in medical and science journals. Of course, when the research pertained to autism and vaccines, their papers always towed the CDC's party line, and the CDC invariably referenced a number of Thorsen's published studies to buttress its case that vaccines have no link to autism. Moreover, Thorsen's studies have been cited in a myriad of cases to deny family's compensation in Vaccine Court.

Dr. Thorsen ultimately built a research empire that the CDC funded to the tune of $16 million. Although he performed the vast majority of his research in Denmark, Dr. Thorsen, acquired the following lofty titles in the US:

- Research Professor, Department of Epidemiology, Rollins School of Public Health, Emory University.

- Associate, Department of Epidemiology, Johns Hopkins University

- CDC appointed principal investigator on the "Epidemiologic studies of reproductive and developmental outcome"

Despite the massive amounts of money and bountiful accolades that were showered upon Dr. Thorsen, he couldn't help himself from embezzling $2 million dollars from the CDC. In 2011, Dr. Thorsen was indicted on 13 counts of wire fraud and 9 counts of money laundering. Facing 260 years in prison and over $20 million in fines, Dr. Thorsen went on the lam and he's still on the lam. It's rather perplexing that Dr. Thorsen has managed to elude an ostensible dragnet by the Department of Justice, the CIA, the FBI, the NSA and all the other international law enforcement agencies for four years.

As Dr. Thorsen was a fugitive from justice, a Danish study published in 2013, "Recurrence of Autism Spectrum Disorders in Full- and Half-Siblings and Trends Over Time: A Population-Based Cohort Study," in the *Journal of the American Medical Association Pediatrics*, found that autism rates in Demark actually declined after thimerosal was banned, which was in direct contradiction to Dr. Thorsen's highly touted study published in *Pediatrics* in 2003.[6]

Dr. Thorsen was a liar, a cheat, and a thief, so the results of all his studies should be called into question, but the CDC still uses those studies to deny a relationship between thimerosal and autism, and the Vaccine Court uses them to deny compensation to victims of vaccine injuries.

---

6   Grønborg TK, Schendel DE, Parner ET. Recurrence of autism spectrum disorders in full- and Half siblings and trends over time: A population based cohort study. JAMA Pediatrics. 2013 Oct; 167(10): 947-53. PMID 23959427.

CHAPTER EIGHT

THE GEIERS LONG DAY'S JOURNEY INTO NIGHT

A t the House's Committee on Oversight and Government Reform's hearings on autism in 2002 officials from the CDC and FDA dipped and dodged questions with regards to an association between thimerosal and autism, but the congressmen were able to receive assurances from the CDC that independent researchers would be able to access the CDC's Vaccine Safety Datalink or VSD. The VSD is a collaborative project between the CDC's Immunization Safety Office and nine health care organizations (HMOs) that was started in 1990 to evaluate the adverse side effects of vaccines. The VSD uses electronic health data from each HMO that includes the type of vaccine that was given to each patient, date of vaccination, and other vaccinations given on the same day. The data in the VSD is considered to be more accurate than VAERS data, because health care professionals corroborate the former, and anyone can file reports online with VAERS. Keeping in mind that only one percent of Serious Adverse Events (SAE) are reported to VAERS.[1] For many years the CDC had refused to release data regarding adverse reactions to vaccines, especially data that demonstrates the culpability of thimerosal in neurological developmental disorders and autism or

---

1   http://vaers.hhs.gov/about/faqs#who_reports.

allow independent researchers to access the VSD. But Mark Geier, MD, PhD, and his son, David, had been relentless in their quest to access the VSD.

The Geiers have been outspoken critics of vaccines that contain thimerosal, and they have published scores of peer-reviewed articles that are primarily related to vaccines and their harmful effects. One study that the Geiers conducted demonstrated that thimerosal is 300 times more harmful to the brain than the bacteria in the vaccines that it's designed to eliminate.[2] Another study by the Geiers cited a viable thimerosal alternative that is far more effective as an antibacterial, but it doesn't have the harmful side effects to the brain as thimerosal.[3] Unfortunately, Mark and David Geier are salient examples of two highly respected scientists who have challenged the establishment about the safety of vaccines, and they've been publicly crucified.

The governor of Maryland appointed Dr. Mark Geier to the Maryland Commission on Autism. Dr. Geier's appointment has significantly improved the quality of life for autistic children in that state. Shortly thereafter, the Geiers developed a scientifically unproven yet effective therapy for severely autistic children. Unfortunately, their treatment gave the Maryland Medical Board all the rope it needed to hang the Geier's, but I'll discuss that later in the subsequent chapter.

Mark Geier was born in 1948, a native to Washington, D.C. He attended George Washington University in Washington, D.C. on a full NCAA division I tennis scholarship. Throughout his storied tennis career, he won 47 United States Tennis Association Mid-Atlantic Section Championships in 10 different categories. One of his noted accomplishments is receiving the United States Tennis Associa-

2   Geier DA, Jordan SK, Geier MR. The relative toxicity of compounds used as preservatives in vaccines and biologics. Med Sci Monit 2010 May; 16(5): SR21-7. PMID 20424565.
3   Geier DA, Sykes LK, Geier MR. A review of thimerosal (merothiolate) and it's ethylmercury breakdown Product: specific historical Considerations regarding safety and effectiveness. J Toxicol Environ Health Crit Rev, 2007 December; 10(8): 575-96. PMID 18049924.
        Study referenced in Geier's paper: Lowe I, Southern J. The antimicrobial activity of phenoxyethanol in vaccines. Lett Appl Microbiol 1994 February; 18(2): 115-6.

tion's number one ranking in mixed doubles in 1977 with his wife, Anne Geier, who was an extremely accomplished tennis player too. Anne won 57 United States Tennis Association Mid-Atlantic Section Championships in 13 different categories. As a mixed doubles team, Mark and Anne have set records for over 40 years.

Mark Geier's impressive accomplishments on the tennis court are only surmounted by his academic and professional accomplishments. He received a bachelors of science in zoology from Georgetown University. He also received a doctorate in genetics and a medical degree from Georgetown University. The National Institutes of Health employed Dr. Geier for 10 years. In 1969, Dr. Geier was a student researcher at the NIH in the Laboratory of General and Comparative Biochemistry division. Within four years, he became a research geneticist and a staff fellow at the NIH. Dr. Geier then ascended to a professional staff member at the NIH. He is also a fellow of the American College of Medical Genetics and served as a Professor at Johns Hopkins University.

Dr. Geier has published numerous scientific papers in his illustrious career. In 1971, he co-authored a paper that was published in *Nature* regarding research that documented the first successful genetic engineering experiment involving bacteriophage lambda, a virus that infects bacteria such as E coli and facilitates the processing of glucose in people who suffer from galactosemia, a disorder that affects how the body processes the simple sugar galactose.[4] Dr. Geier's research on this subject received praise and accolades from both *Newsweek* and the *New York Times*.

Dr. Geier's son, David, is a graduate of the University of Maryland with a B.A., in Biology. The father and son team have published scores of peer-reviewed articles that are primarily related to vaccines and genetics. The Geier's articles are co-authored by credible professionals in their respective fields of expertise, and they were the first independent researchers to access the VSD, the CDC's vault of secrets.

---

4   Merril C.R., Geier M.R., Petricceiani J.C. Bacterial virus gene expression in human cells. Nature. 1971 Oct 8; 233(5319): 398-400. PMID: 4940436.

Theoretically, America's Health Insurance Plans manages the VSD, because, in 2002, the CDC entered into a ten year, $195 million contract with the Health Insurance Association of America, whereby the latter would manage the VSD. A subsequent merger between the Health Insurance Association of America and the American Association of Health Plans in 2003 created America's Health Insurance Plans. Karen Ignagni is the president and chief executive officer of America's Health Insurance Plans and former president and chief executive officer of Health Insurance Association of America. She is essentially the voice for the health insurance industry, and she's considered one of the most effective lobbyists in Washington, DC.

Despite the tremendous power exercised by Ignagni and America's Health Insurance Plans, its management of the VSD appears to be a smokescreen. As I've previously mentioned, the Reverend Sykes' son was diagnosed with ASD, and she concluded that his autism was the result of mercury poisoning via a vaccine. The Reverend Sykes sued GlaxoSmithKline, and her attorneys deposed America's Health Insurance Plans' VSD project manager, who testified that the CDC had ongoing involvement in the regulation of independent researchers accessing the VSD. So, ultimately, the America's Health Insurance Plans' management of the VSD, at least regarding independent researchers, is only theoretical.

The Geiers' initial request to gain access to the VSD predated the public announcement that allowed independent researchers to access to the VSD. At the time of their initial request, the chief of CDC's National Immunization Safety program, Dr. Robert Chen, informed the Geiers that the CDC would grant them access to the VSD with a written request. After waiting nearly three weeks, the Geiers received a letter in response from Dr. Chen and the CDC, but it wasn't the response they anticipated. Dr. Chen wrote that now that the CDC had announced making the VSD publicly accessible, they would have to submit an entirely different proposal.

The Geiers then began the process of filing their new proposal. They stated in their proposal that they had conducted several studies on vaccine safety analyzing the VAERS data and their intention was to conduct a comparable analysis of the VSD. After giving Geiers the runaround, the CDC concluded it required additional clarification about their proposal. The CDC wanted to know their exact analytical methods and statistical methods and also their precise hypothesis regarding vaccines. Their initial request was one page, but to satisfy the CDC's latter demands their request ballooned to over 200 pages.

In December of 2002, as the Geiers' request to access the VSD database was mired in red tape, the House of Representatives' Committee on Oversight and Government reform held its 2002 hearing on the safety of vaccines, which I've previously discussed, and both Mark and David testified before the hearing. In the middle of Mark Geier's testimony, Representative Burton asked him if he had been granted access to the VSD database. Dr. Geier replied that he hadn't been granted access, and then he discussed the CDC's seemingly endless gauntlet of hoops he and his son had had to jump through with no end in sight. Burton applied pressure to the CDC, and later in the month, the Geiers received a letter from the CDC stating that their proposal had been approved.

Despite the CDC approving the Geiers' request in December, they had to continue to jump through a variety of hoops. By February the Geier's were becoming exceedingly frustrated with the CDC, and they filed a series of additional requests. In addition to requesting to analyze data for their own studies in the VSD, they sought to reanalyze data from previously published studies. The Geiers received some very interesting responses from the CDC in their request to access the Verstraeten study data and other studies they sought to analyze. The CDC informed the Geiers that it had the data, but the data was stored on obsolete media, so they wouldn't be able to access it. The Geiers responded that they could access the data even if it was stored on obsolete media. The CDC then informed the Geiers that the media was damaged, and the Geiers replied that they would repair the media. Finally, the CDC said that the data had been lost.

The CDC required that the Geiers to receive permission from the respective HMOs whose data was in the VSD. Because each HMO in the VSD database had its own policies regarding human subject protocols and patient confidentiality, all proposals needed to be submitted in a specific format for each HMO.

The Geiers' first attempts to receive HMO approval began early in 2003. They were able to contact the Institutional Review Boards (IRBs) at Group Health Cooperative, Northwestern Kaiser, Northern California Kaiser, Southern California Kaiser, Kaiser Colorado, and UCLA-Harbor.

The UCLA-Harbor HMO didn't even have an IRB and eventually contracted a private company to act as its IRB, and it required the Geiers to divide their research requests into 22 separate proposals. UCLA-Harbor's ad hoc IRB reviewed each of the Geiers' proposals one application at a time. Moreover, the IRB was unwilling to participate in prearranged conference calls with congress to resolve the various issues the Geiers encountered.

Despite the run around of the CDC, the Geiers continued to persevere in their quest to access the VSD. As the Geiers were mired in the CDC's seemingly perpetual state of red tape, in May of 2003 the House of Representatives' Subcommittee on Human Rights and Wellness released a report entitled "Mercury in Medicine – Taking Unnecessary Risks." The House's report concluded that the thimerosal in vaccines was likely related to the autism epidemic. The last paragraph of the 81-page report stated:

> Thimerosal used as a preservative in vaccines in likely related to the autism epidemic. This epidemic in all probability may have been prevented or curtailed had the FDA not been asleep at the switch regarding the lack of safety data regarding injected thimerosal and the sharp rise of infant exposure to this known neurotoxin. Our public health agencies' failure to act is indicative of institutional malfeasance for self-protection and misplaced protectionism of the pharmaceutical industry.

In addition to "Mercury in Medicine – Taking Unnecessary Risks" placing the onus of the autism epidemic on the failure of government agencies, U.S. Representative Dave Weldon wrote a letter to the Director of the CDC of behalf of the Geiers that put additional heat on the CDC to permit the Geiers to access the VSD.

By June of 2003, the Geiers were approved by the IRBs of four HMO's to access the VSD database. The Geiers subsequently contacted the CDC, and informed it that four IRBs had granted them full access to data in the VSD. But the CDC countered that the Geier's access would be contingent on the information that they sought to access.

The Geiers and the CDC eventually overcame their impasse a week before the Geiers were scheduled to visit the VSD research data center. Shortly after the Geiers were given the green light to access the VSD database, they were informed that the CDC would charge them a slight admission fee to enter the building. The Geier's were quoted an initial flat rate of $3,208.85.

Although Congress requested that the Geiers investigate the VSD data, they were still required to submit a certified check to access the government data. Naturally, the Geiers attempted to have the fee waived, but the CDC was implacable, so the Geiers coughed up the cash.

The CDC granted the Geiers a minimum of two days and a maximum of ten days to access the VSD data. Shortly after the Geiers were finally granted access to the VSD database, the CDC informed them that the data was configured in SAS, which was a rather archaic and obsolete software language. The Geiers weren't proficient in SAS, and the CDC mandated that a programmer who was capable of deciphering SAS couldn't accompany them. But the Geiers appealed to their congressional allies, and the CDC eventually relented to have a programmer accompany the Geiers when they accessed the VSD database.

The Geiers were on the precipice of finally accessing the VSD database, but they had to find a programmer who was capable of deciphering SAS. After a series of frantic phone calls, they found the father of an autistic child who was an expert computer programmer. Although he wasn't proficient in SAS, he was a quick study, and he managed to master the rudiments of SAS in a couple of weeks.

The Geiers' sheer tenacity had enabled them to circumnavigate the CDC's vast labyrinth, and they finally had all the pieces of the puzzle in place to analyze the VSD database. The Geier's contacted the CDC and made arrangements to access the VSD database on two days in October of 2003.

The VSD database contains data compiled from surveillance on approximately 500,000 children from birth through six years of age, but the surveillance data doesn't include the patients' names, addresses, zip codes, state of residence, phone numbers, HMO affiliation, or center of examination. Despite this fact, the CDC mandated that if the Geiers performed a search on specific vaccines and their outcomes, and the Geiers search results had less than five results, then the entire search would be whited out: The rationale the CDC offered for its mandate was that if the Geiers had search results with less than five patients, the Geiers would then be able to extrapolate the identity of the children in the VSD, which was rather absurd because the VSD provided no personal information on the children. The CDC's ground rules for the Geiers were quite different than its ground rules for Thomas Vertsraeten, who was allowed a minimum of 18 results for every search.

The VSD database was located in the National Center for Health Statistic in Huntsville, Maryland. The Geiers rendezvoused with their programmer and ally at the Huntsville facility, which was an obscure, non-descriptive brick building without even a sign. The data center may have lacked signs, but it compensated for its lack of insignias with security. Indeed, the building's security made the TSA gauntlet of an airport appear as a lark.

The Geiers were greeted by armed guards at the door and thoroughly searched. They were also assigned a monitor whose task was to mirror their every move. The CDC had thrown so many obstacles at the Geiers that it would have been next to impossible for them to conduct a reasonable analysis of the VSD data, but the CDC hadn't counted on the Geiers gleaning assistance from a world-class expert on that particular system: The CDC's monitor was a biostatician with a PhD, and she just happened to be sympathetic to their cause.

She enabled the Geiers to glean data that corroborated their earlier research, demonstrating that there was indeed an association between thimerosal and autism. Over the course of two days, and despite a myriad of obstacles, the Geiers were able to replicate the research they had conducted on the VAERS database. They analyzed children receiving the thimerosal containing DTaP vaccine and compared that data to children who received the thimerosal free DTaP vaccine and found an association between thimerosal and autism. The Geiers also found that children who received four vaccinations by 18 months of childhood had a statistically significant higher rate of autism.

In January of 2004, the Geiers were granted access to the VSD for a second session. Apparently, it had occurred to the CDC that the Geiers received assistance from their first monitor, because she had been replaced during their second visit to the VSD. In fact, the CDC now assigned two monitors to the Geiers, and they proved to be less than helpful, and the second session was a disaster.

The two monitors started to impose random, ad hoc rules on the Geiers. If there was one piece of data on a printout that they claimed the Geier's couldn't see, they would whiteout the entire printout. Finally, David Geier phoned Representative Weldon's office, requesting support. But the CDC told the Geiers that members of Weldon's staff wouldn't be allowed to enter the building, because they hadn't been approved by the IRBs of the various HMO's whose data was in the VSD. Consequently, the Geiers weren't able to peruse any meaningful data on their return trip to the VSD.

Although the Geiers second sojourn to the VSD had resulted in nil, they were nonetheless excited to share their VSD results with the Institute of Medicine's "Immunization Safety Review: Vaccines and Autism" meeting on the February 9th, 2004. The Institute of Medicine was founded by the

National Academy of Sciences and, according to its charter: "The Institute of Medicine was established in 1970 by the National Academy of Sciences to secure the services of eminent members of appropriate professions in the examination of policy matters pertaining to the health of the public. The Institute acts under the responsibility given to the National Academy of Sciences by its congressional charter to be an adviser to the federal government and, upon its own initiative, to identify issues of medical care, research, and education."

For the meeting, the Institute of Medicine assembled an array of scientists and researchers, including the Geiers, who would present scientific findings on the relationship between vaccines and autism, and a "review committee" would assess the data. The review committee was composed experts in the filed of medicine who heralded from grand academic institutions – like Harvard and Johns Hopkins – and they also had a variety of lofty degrees.

The Institute of Medicine's charter seems fair and unbiased, but politics can obfuscate its ideals, and the 2004 meeting, "Immunization Safety Review: Vaccines and Autism" hearing wasn't fair or unbiased. In fact, Representative Weldon had been allotted 15 minutes to dispense introductory comments before the meeting's scientific presentations, and his remarks clearly delineated that he believed the meeting was little more than a sham.

At the meeting, the Geiers presentation was preceded by the presentation of Robert Davis, MD, MPH, who hailed from the University of Washington's Departments of Pediatrics and Center for Health Studies and Epidemiology. Dr. Davis' presentation was essentially a frontal assault on the Geiers' research, but it lacked veracity. When the Geiers perused the VSD database, they concluded that infants receiving four vaccinations by 18 months of age were much more susceptible to autism, but Davis was reporting on infants who were two months of age and hadn't received at least four vaccinations, and he didn't find a correlation between vaccinations and autism.

All the presenters at the February 2004 Institute of Medicine meeting, with the exception of the Geiers, concluded that there wasn't a link between vaccines and autism, and the final report of the meeting essentially concluded that there wasn't a link between vaccines and autism, so the vast shadowy labyrinth of government entities and pharmaceutical interests that the Geiers were fighting certainly won that battle.

To add insult to injury, within one week of the Geier's presentation at the Institute of Medicine, the CDC sent letters to the various HMO's whose data was in the VSD that accused the Geiers of merging datasets and breaching patient confidentiality. The CDC's accusations were rather absurd, because the VSD data didn't include patient names, addresses, zip codes, state of residence, phone numbers, HMO affiliation, or center of examination.

Despite the CDC's baseless accusations, its letters prompted the HMOs to withdraw their permission to permit the Geiers to access the VSD. The Geiers then sent letters to the HMOs categorically denying the CDC's accusations, and the HMOs eventually reinstated their authorization to allow the Geiers to access the VSD.

As the Geiers were reeling from the Institute of Medicine meeting and the CDC's underhanded tactics to deny them access to the VSD, the U.S. Office of Special Counsel, which is an independent federal investigative and prosecutorial agency, forwarded a myriad of disclosures to congress about safety concerns regarding childhood vaccines. The disclosures contended that the CDC and FDA colluded with pharmaceutical companies at the Simpsonwood conference in June 2000 to prevent the release of the actual data in Vertsraeten study. And in a seeming about face, the Institute of Medicine published a 2005 report entitled, "Vaccine Safety Research, Data Access, and Public Trust," which criticized the CDC's and *America's Health Insurance Plans'* stranglehold on the VSD data. The report made recommendations that would broaden the guidelines for external researchers accessing the VSD.

The Institute of Medicine's report and pressure from Congress finally loosened the CDC's and *America's Health Insurance Plans'* stranglehold on the VSD data, which enabled Heather Young, PhD, a professor of epidemiology at George Washington University and the Geiers to gain access to the VSD without the constraints that had been formerly placed on the Geiers. In 2008, Dr. Young and Geiers had an article published in the *Journal of Neurological Sciences*, "Thimerosal Exposure in Infants and Neurodevelopmental Disorders: An Assessment of Computerized Medical Records in the Vaccine Safety Datalink," which was the result of their VSD data mining.[5]

The study conducted by Dr. Young and the Geiers assessed the possible associations between neurodevelopmental disorders and exposure to mercury from thimerosal-containing vaccines by examining 278,624 subjects in the VSD who were born between 1990 and 1996 and received their first oral polio vaccination by 3 months of age. Although the polio vaccine doesn't contain thimerosal, it was chosen because this vaccine was the only vaccine that was consistently administered to all children during the timeframe of the study.

Dr. Young and the Geiers also assessed additional vaccines that these infants received before seven months of age and before 13 months of age. The routine childhood vaccines of interest were Haemophilus Influenza Type b (Hib), hepatitis B vaccine, Diphtheria-Tetanus-acellular-Pertussis (DTaP), and the whole-cell Diphtheria-Tetanus-Pertussis (DTP). The DTaP, DTP, Hib vaccines each contained 25 micrograms of mercury per dose, and the hepatitis B vaccine contained 12.5 micrograms of mercury per dose.

Dr. Young and the Geiers found the following for infants who received an aggregate of 100 micrograms of mercury before the age of seven months:

• 2.87-fold increase in autism

---

5 Young HA, Geier DA, Geier MR. Thimerosal exposure in infants and neurodevelopmental disorders: an assesment of computerized medical records in the vaccine safety datalink. J Neurol Sci. 2008 Aug 15; 271(1-2): 110-8. PMID 18482737.

• 2.44-fold increase in autism spectrum disorders

• 1.73-fold increase in developmental and learning disorders

• 2.27-fold increase in emotional disorders

• 3.39-fold increase in tics

Dr. Young and the Geiers found the following for infants who received an aggregate of 100 micrograms of mercury before the age of 13 months:

• 2.62-fold increase in autism

• 2.2-fold increase in autism spectrum disorders

• 1.81-fold increase in developmental and learning disorders

• 2.91-fold increase in emotional disorders

• 4.11-fold increase in tics

Clearly, the results of Dr. Young and the Geiers study demonstrate that infants who received an aggregate of 100 micrograms of mercury via vaccines are significantly prone to autism, autism spectrum disorders, developmental and learning disorders, emotional disorders, and tics. But, unfortunately, the Geiers access of the VSD would mark the beginning of their doom.

CHAPTER NINE

LUPRON THERAPY AND THE GEIERS DARK NIGHT OF THE SOUL

As Dr. Young and the Geiers crunched the numbers of the 278,624 infants in the VSD, they not only noticed a significant increase in neurodevelopmental disorders for infants who received 100 micrograms of mercury via vaccines, but they also noticed a correlation between thimerosal containing vaccines and premature puberty.

But after Dr. Young and the Geiers published their paper linking neurodevelopmental disorders in infants to thimerosal in the *Journal of Neurological Sciences* in 2008, the medical industrial complex closed ranks, and they found it nearly impossible to publish the additional revelations that they had gleaned from the VSD in science journals that were published in the US. Ever relentless, though, the Geiers and Dr. Young published a 2010 article, "Thimerosal Exposure & Increasing Trends of Premature Puberty in the Vaccine Safety Datalink," in the *Indian Journal of Medical Research*, which demonstrated the link between thimerosal and premature puberty.[1]

---

1   Geier DA, Young HA, Geier MR. Thimerosal exposure & increasing trends of premature puberty in the vaccine safety datalink. Indian J Med Res. 2010 Apr; 131: 500-7. PMID 20424300.

In the article, Dr. Young and the Geiers analyzed 278,624 infants in the VSD, and they found a 5.58-fold increase in premature puberty for infants who received 100 micrograms of thimerosal before seven months of age and a 6.45-fold increase in premature puberty for infants who received 100 micrograms of thimerosal before 13 months of age.

Prior to the 2010 article published in the *Indian Journal of Medical Research*, the Geiers had hypothesized that many autistic children had abnormally high testosterone levels. The Geiers first became interested in this question after coming across a study by Dr. Boyd Haley, who was the chairman of the Department of Chemistry at the University of Kentucky, which showed that testosterone and mercury created a synergy that greatly enhanced the destructive biological powers of mercury on brain neurons. The Geiers explicated their theory regarding testosterone, mercury, and autism in a 2005 article that was published in *Medical Hypotheses*:

> In considering mercury toxicity, it has previously been shown that testosterone significantly potentiates mercury toxicity, whereas estrogen is protective. Examination of autistic children has shown that the severity of autistic disorders correlates with the amount of testosterone present in the amniotic fluid, and an examination of a case-series of autistic children has shown that some have plasma testosterone levels that were significantly elevated in comparison to neurotypical control children.[2]

In 2006, the Geiers published an article in the journal of *Hormone Research* that evaluated the testosterone levels in 16 children with ASD under the age of 11, and they found that all of the children had significantly elevated testosterone levels.[3]

In addition to the Geiers, several subsequent researchers have found a link between ASD and testosterone. A 2014

2   Geier MR, Geier DA. The potential impotence of steroids in the treatment of autistic spectrum disorders and other disorders involving mercury toxicity. Med Hypotheses. 2005; 64(5): 946-54. PMID 15780490.

3   Geier DA, Geier MR, A clinical laboratory evaluation of methionine cycle-transsulfuration and androgen pathwaymarkers in children with autistic disorders. Hormone Research 2006; 66(4): 182-8. PMID 16825783.

article published in the *International Journal of Adolescent Medicine* also assessed androgen levels (testosterone is an androgen) in autistic children versus healthy controls.[4] The researchers compared 20 healthy children to 30 children with ASD, and they too found that androgen levels were significantly elevated in autistic children. Moreover, androgen levels increased with autistic severity.

A 2011 article published in the science journal *Psychoneuroendocrinology* assessed 128 participants, 58 of whom had a diagnosis of Asperger Syndrome or high functioning autism and 70 participants who were age- and IQ-matched controls, and the researchers found that the group with ASD had significantly elevated levels of androstenedione, which is a precursor to the formation of testosterone.[5]

A 2009 article published in the *British Journal of Psychology* found that children who were exposed to elevated testosterone levels even in the womb had a greater susceptibility to autistic-like symptoms.[6] The researchers evaluated 235 pairs of mothers and children over eight years, and the children periodically received questionnaires that measured their autistic traits. None of the children in the study received an autism diagnosis, but the researchers found that the children who had been exposed to higher testosterone levels in the womb – measured via amniocentesis during pregnancy – had a greater chance of displaying autism-associated traits.

The Geiers felt that they had a very important piece of the ASD puzzle when their research found that testosterone levels were significantly elevated in children with ASD. Prior to the Geiers research, scientists couldn't account for the fact that ASD was four to five times more prevalent in boys than girls. A 2007 study in Hormones and Behavior also found that girls with autism spectrum conditions (ASC) had higher levels of

4   El-Baz F: et al. Hyperandrogenemia in male autistic children and adolescents: relation to disease and severity. Int J Adolesc Med Health. 2014; 26(1): 79-84. PMID 23612632.

5   Ruta L: et al. Increased serum androstenedione in adults with autism spectrum disorders. Psychoneuroendocrinology: 2011 Sep; 36(8): 1154-63. PMID 21398041.

6   Auyeung B: et al. Fetal testosterone and autistic traits. Br J Psychology 2009 Feb; 100(pt 1): 1-22. PMID: 18547459.

testosterone. Additionally, compared to controls, significantly more women with ASC had higher rates of androgen-related conditions such as Poly-cystic Ovarian Syndrome, hirsutism, and family history of hormone-related cancers.[7]

In addition to confirming their hypothesis that children with ASD have higher levels of testosterone, the Geier's study that was published in Neurochemical Research found that children with ASD had decreased levels of glutathione. Glutathione is the most abundant amino acid that is produced naturally in the body, and it is considered to be the "mother of all antioxidants." Glutathione contains a sulfur chemical group that acts like flypaper and many of the toxins circulating in the body stick to it, including free radicals and toxins like mercury and other heavy metals.

People take oral glutathione for treating cataracts and glaucoma, and for preventing aging, asthma, cancer, heart disease, hepatitis, liver disease, diseases that weaken the body's defense system (including AIDS and chronic fatigue syndrome), memory loss, Alzheimer's disease, osteoarthritis, and Parkinson's disease. Glutathione is also used for maintaining the immune system and fighting metal and drug poisoning.

Healthcare providers also give patients intravenous injections of glutathione for preventing anemia in kidney patients undergoing hemodialysis treatment, preventing kidney problems after heart bypass surgery, treating Parkinson's disease, improving blood flow and decreasing clotting in individuals with hardening of the arteries, treating diabetes, and preventing the toxic side effects of chemotherapy.

Glutathione is also the body's primary molecule for mercury detoxification. Glutathione binds to mercury, and it prevents mercury from interacting with cell proteins, such as enzymes responsible for energy and neurotransmitter production and other tissues. The glutathione/mercury complexes are carried to the liver to be excreted through the bile and intestines or to the kidneys where the glutathione/mercury complexes are excreted through the urine.

7   Ingudomnukul E: et al. Elevated rates of testosterone-related disorders in women with autism spectrum conditions. Horm Behavior. 2007 May; 51(5): 597-604. PMID 17462645.

The Geier's research regarding children with ASD having higher levels of testosterone and lower levels of glutathione has been replicated by a number of researchers. A 2014 article published in the science journal *Behavioral and Brain Functions* assessed 52 patients with autism spectrum disorder, and the study's subjects had significantly higher levels of mercury and lower levels of glutathione compared with the controls.[8] The investigators wrote that their "study confirms earlier studies that implicate toxic metal accumulation as a consequence of impaired detoxification in autism and provides insight into the etiological mechanism of autism."

As the Geiers started researching the nexus between glutathione and testosterone, they found a 1976 article published in the European *Biochimica et Biophysica Acta* (Molecular and Cell Biology of Lipids) demonstrating that a deficiency of glutathione impedes an enzyme that restricts the production of testosterone.[9] Thus, a glutathione deficiency produces a proliferation of testosterone in the body. The Geiers also found a 1968 article that was published in a European science journal, *Acta Crystallographica*, that shows how mercury binds to testosterone to produce mercury-testosterone "lattices" that are difficult for the body's enzymes to breakdown and evacuate.[10]

According to the Geiers, the mercury-testosterone lattices are resistant to chelation, which is a medical procedure that involves the administration of chelating agents to remove heavy metals from the body. Chelation therapy has a long history of use in clinical toxicology and remains in use for some very specific medical treatments. In chelation therapy, a chelating agent is delivered intravenously, and the chelating agent seeks out and binds to minerals in the bloodstream. Once the medication binds to the min-

---

8   Altaf Alabdali, Laila Al-Ayadhi, Afaf EL-Ansary. A key role for an impaired detoxification mechanism in the etiology and severity of autism spectrum disorders. Behavior Brain Funct. 2014 April; vol 10: 14. PMCID: PMC 4017810.
9   Ryan R.A., Carrol J. Studies on a 3 beta-hydroxysteroid sulphotransferase from rat liver. Biochim Biophys Acta. 1976 Apr 8; 429(2): 391-401. PMID: 4129.
10   Cooper A., Gopalakrishna E.M., Norton D.A., The crystal structure and absolute configuration of the 2:1 complex between testosterone and mercuric chloride. Acta Crystallogr B. 1968 July 15; 24(7): 935-41. PMID: 5756987.

erals, it creates a compound that leaves the body through urine.

The Geiers theorized that if they were able to temporarily shut down testosterone production in children with ASD, it might release the trapped stores of mercury, so they began to contemplate administering Lupron to children with ASD. Lupron is a drug that inhibits the body's ability to produce testosterone, and it is used to treat precocious puberty, prostate cancer, and estrogen-dependent conditions such as endometriosis or uterine fibroids. Lupron has also been tested as a treatment for sex offenders who volunteer for testosterone suppression in order to gain parole.

By the time the Geiers had started to contemplate the use of Lupron for ASD, they had become major activists in the credo that mercury was partially responsible for the autistic epidemic, which brought them into contact with other activists, including the Reverend Lisa K. Sykes. As I mentioned earlier in the book, Reverend Sykes' book, *Sacred Spark*, was revelatory to me concerning mercury's link to autism. *Sacred Spark* recounted the difficulties she faced when her son, Wesley, had been diagnosed with ASD, and she concluded that his autism was the result of mercury poisoning via a vaccine.

When the Geiers discussed Lupron therapy for ASD with the Reverend Sykes, their theory resonated with her, because her nine-year-old autistic son was definitely experiencing precocious puberty: He was having erections in the shower, masturbating, sporting pubic hair, and he had a two-inch growth spurt over the previous year. The Reverend Sykes had tried chelation on her son, but it didn't have the desired affect of abating his autism. After the Reverend Sykes had Wesley's condition of precocious puberty confirmed by his physician, she decided to give the Geiers' Lupron protocol a shot, and her son was their first patient for their Lupron protocol.

As the first patient, the Geiers were surprised to find that a Lupron shot that should have brought Wesley's testosterone levels from 25 to 0 merely reduced it to 18. As Wesley continued to receive Lupron, his mother noted significant changes in his behavior. Wesley's hyperactivity was greatly reduced, he was able to swing on a swing, and he began to make verbalizations. Wesley is now twelve years old, and he is extremely calm, affectionate, interactive and able to type at keyboard. His inappropriate sexual behavior has also vanished, and he has a fairly good grasp of his emotions and what is happening around him.

Wesley was one of the initial 11 patients with ASD and precocious puberty that the Geiers treated with Lupron. The 11 patients were on Lupron therapy for a minimum of 2 months and a maximum of 7 months, and, after their Lupron treatments, they were given chelation therapy to remove the vestiges of their mercury poisoning.

Dr. Geier conducted an extensive physical exam and various tests on the patients before their Lupron therapy and after their Lupron therapy. He evaluated the patients' clinical symptoms and behaviors of precocious puberty such as early growth spurt, early secondary sexual changes, body and facial hair, and aggressive behaviors. The Geiers also administered the Autism Treatment Evaluation Checklist (ATEC) to the patients prior to treatment and after treatment. The ATEC quantitatively evaluates (using a numeric scoring system) skills in a number of areas, including speech language/communication, sociability, sensory/cognitive awareness, and behavior. Laboratory tests were also conducted on each subject at baseline and at approximately 3 months of treatment.

All of the patients experienced a significant decrease in their testosterone levels that was accompanied by significant reductions in their clinical symptoms of precocious puberty such as early secondary sexual changes, body and facial hair, and aggressive behaviors. According to the ATEC, the patients showed significant improvement in the areas of sociability, cognitive awareness, and behavior. The patients had an overall improvement from the 70th percentile of autistic severity at the onset of Lupron treatment to the 40–49th percentile of severity at the end of the study. Moreover, specific subjects had independent assessments by school evaluators, who were not aware of the treatment status of the child, and the school evaluators found significant improvements in general school skills and in the frequency and severity of disruptive and oppositional behavior. Additionally, the Geiers found that the treatment didn't adversely affect kidney, thyroid or liver function.

Dr. Geier ultimately treated 200 hundred children with precocious puberty and ASD with Lupron, and, overall, the patients he treated had considerable improvements in autistic behavior such as better sleep patterns, improvements in attention and hyperactivity, and increased socialization. And, importantly, none of the patients experienced severe or lasting adverse events or conditions.

The Geiers were elated by their results, and Dr. Geier ultimately applied for medical licenses in California, Florida, Hawaii, Illinois, Indiana, Kentucky, Missouri, New Jersey, Virginia, and Washington, where he started opening clinics to treat precocious puberty, ASD patients with Lupron. Lupron is an expensive drug that costs $5,000 to $6,000 a month, but insurance companies will cover the cost of Lupron if it's used to treat precocious puberty.

Although the Geiers were experiencing phenomenal success with Lupron, they had made enemies – powerful enemies – over the years. The Geiers had demonstrated a link between mercury and autism in several studies, they had been unyielding in their quest to access the VSD to demonstrate a link between mercury and autism, and Dr. Geier had testified in about 100 cases in the Vaccine Court regarding the deleterious effects of thimerosal. So Dr. Geier was much more than a thorn in the side of the CDC and Big Pharma – he was a hemorrhaging wound. Moreover, the CDC had declared that there wasn't a viable treatment for autism, and the Geiers were once again proving the CDC to be wrong. Unfortunately, the Geiers successful treatment protocol for autistic children was a ticking time bomb for their careers.

The outright attacks against Dr. Geier commenced in August of 2006, when a woman named Lisa Randall filed a complaint against Dr. Geier with the Maryland Department of Health and Mental Hygiene. Randall's complaint was very bizarre indeed, because she wasn't a parent of a child with ASD who Dr. Geier had treated with Lupron. In fact, none of her children have ASD. At the time she filed her complaint against Dr. Geier, Randall was a "policy consultant" for the Immunization Action Coalition, which is funded by the CDC and Big Pharma and is a major mouthpiece concerning the good works of vaccines.

As the basis of her complaint, Randall cited the posts of Kathleen Seidel, who repeatedly attacked the Geiers on her blog. Seidel is the mother of an autistic child, and her blog makes references to autism being a "gift" and it excoriates people who think otherwise. Given that the Geiers don't look upon autism as a gift, it's woefully obvious that Seidel and the Geiers would have conflicting views on autism.

In 2008, a physician who had referred a patient to Dr. Geier filed a second complaint against him. Although the physician filing the complaint didn't feel a Lupron course of treatment was appropriate for the child, the patient's parents were completely satisfied with the results of Lupron therapy, and they refused to file a complaint against Dr. Geier.

A third complaint was filed against Dr. Geier in 2008. The woman who filed the complaint brought her child to Dr. Geier's clinic in 2005 for an evaluation. Dr. Geier instructed the woman to take her child in for blood work, but she never brought her child to the lab. Three years later, the woman reappeared at the Geiers' clinic, and she said that she wanted to resume the process of starting Lupron therapy on her child. The woman and her child were again sent to the lab for tests. This time she actually showed up at the lab, but, after testing, Dr. Geier never heard from again until her name was identified on the third complaint.

Two of the three complaints lodged against Dr. Geier were dubious, and none of the parents whose autistic children had been treated by the Geiers have ever lodged a complaint against Dr. Geier. Moreover, Dr. Geier was a highly respected physician and scientist, so the complaints against him weren't acted upon ... immediately.

In January of 2011, the Geiers were testifying before United Nations Environment Programme's second session of the Intergovernmental Negotiating Committee on Mercury, and their Lupron protocol for autistic children with precocious puberty was being incorporated by various clinics around the country, but a bad moon was rising for them in Maryland.

The Geiers bad moon came in the form of Dr. Joshua F. Scharfstein who was appointed Secretary of the Maryland Department of Health and Mental Hygiene in January of 2011. Dr. Scharfstein had been a vociferous critic of the Geiers' research, and he's a fellow of the American Academy of Pediatrics, which is an unfaltering supporter of universal vaccinations.

In April of 2011, the Maryland State Board of Physicians suspended Dr. Geier's medical license as an "emergency action." The charges were based on his treatment of autistic children with Lupron, and they included exploiting the parents of autistic children, improper diagnoses, record keeping infractions, etc. In other words, Dr. Geier was being railroaded and the train had now left the station.

In May, Dr. Geier appeared before a hearing of the Maryland State Board of Physicians, and requested that it lift the suspension of his medical license. He presented affidavits from parents thanking him for treating their children. The affidavits also affirmed that the parents had been fully informed and denied their children had been misdiagnosed. Moreover, Dr. Geier presented scientific evidence supporting the Lupron protocol. But the Board wouldn't budge, and it didn't lift Dr. Geiers' suspension.

In September, the Board formally charged Dr. Geier with unprofessional conduct, willfully making false medical reports, failing to file medical reports as required by law, practicing medicine with an unauthorized person (David), grossly over utilizing health services, failing to provide appropriate medical care, and failing to keep adequate medical records.

He had a five-day evidentiary hearing in March of 2012, and, by that time, the train had gathered considerable momentum. A myriad of newspaper articles had reported on his "chemical castration" of children that was predicated on "junk science." Dr. Geier lost the evidentiary hearing in March, and his medical license was revoked. And like falling dominoes, his medical licenses were revoked in California, Florida, Indiana, Kentucky, New Jersey, Texas, Virginia, Washington and Hawaii.

Dr. Geier's story is like that of Greek mythology's Icarus. Icarus flew too close to the sun with wax wings that melted, and he died after plummeting to the Earth. But Dr. Geier's story has a contemporary twist. He ventured too close to a black hole that devours children, parents, and the truth.

CHAPTER TEN

DR. WAKEFIELD'S PUBLIC CRUCIFIXION

Andrew J. Wakefield, MD, like Mark Geier, is an example of a physician speaking out about the deleterious effects of vaccines and enduring a very public crucifixion. Dr. Wakefield was an esteemed British gastroenterologist who received a medical degree from St. Mary's Hospital Medical School, an adjunct of the University of London, in 1981. He hailed from a long lineage of physicians. Indeed, he was the fourth generation of his family to have studied medicine at St. Mary's Hospital Medical School.

Dr. Wakefield pursued a career in gastrointestinal surgery with a particular interest in inflammatory bowel disease (IBD). He became a Fellow of the Royal College of Surgeons in 1985, and a year later, he was awarded a prestigious Welcome Trust Fellowship to study small-intestinal transplantation in Toronto, Canada. The Welcome Trust is a United Kingdom-based charitable foundation dedicated to achieving improvements in health by supporting the "brightest minds." After receiving a Welcome Trust Fellowship, Dr. Wakefield became a Fellow of the Royal College of Pathologists in 2001, and he has published over 140 original scientific articles and book chapters.

Dr. Wakefield assembled a stellar career in medicine ... until he came to the realization that vaccines can cause autism. In 1996, when Dr. Wakefield embarked on this realization, he was employed at London's Royal Free Hospital. On December 20th, 1996, the vagaries of fate intervened on

Wakefield's life, and he attended a meeting sponsored by the Welcome Trust in London.

At the meeting, Dr. John Walker-Smith, the Chairman of Pediatric Gastroenterology at Royal Free Hospital, and a world renowned physician, presented the preliminary results of a study entitled "Entero-Colitis and Disintegrative Disorder Following MMR: A Review of the First Seven Cases," which demonstrated a correlation among children with developmental disorders and gastrointestinal symptoms, who had received the measles, mumps, and rubella (MMR) vaccine. Dr. Walker-Smith's presentation was based upon his review of endoscopic and microscopic findings in the intestinal biopsies of the children. "I wish today," said Dr. Walker-Smith, "to present some preliminary details concerning seven children, all boys who appear to have entro-colitis and disintegrative disorder, probably autism, following MMR . . ." Dr. Walker-Smith's findings were supported by a senior pathologist at the Royal Free Hospital, Dr. Amar Dhillon, an expert on intestinal pathology.

Drs. Wakefield, Dhillon, Walker-Smith and ten of their colleagues ultimately submitted research on 12 children who had received an MMR vaccine to *The Lancet*, one of the most prestigious peer-reviewed medical journals in circulation. *The Lancet* published the article on their research, "Ileal-Lymphoid-Nodular Hyperplasia, Non-Specific Colitis, and Pervasive Developmental Disorder in Children" in February of 1998.[1]

The study's cohort consisted of 12 healthy children who had received the MMR vaccine between 12 and 15 months of age. The children were subsequently afflicted with intestinal abnormalities, and nine of the children had been subsequently afflicted with autism and one suffered from a disintegrative psychosis.

Although *The Lancet* article didn't suggest that children should no longer receive the MMR vaccine, it suggested a possible association between the MMR vaccine and autism that warranted further investigation. However, the study's

---

1   Wakefield A.J., et al. Ileal-lymphoid-nodular hyperplasia, non-specific colitis, and pervasive developmental disorder in children. Lancet 1998 Feb 28; 351(9103): 637–41. PMID: 9500320.

results placed fear in the hearts of the pharmaceutical companies, and seriously undermined the sacred philosophy of Britain's vaccination programs.

Prior to *The Lancet* article's publication, Dr. Wakefield and his fellow co-authors of *The Lancet* article held a press conference. During the press conference, Dr. Wakefield didn't contend that children should stop receiving vaccinations. In fact, he stated that children should continue to receive vaccinations. Moreover, he didn't say that an MMR vaccine was incontrovertibly responsible the autism, but, rather, he maintained that children shouldn't receive the MMR vaccine until further research determined whether or not it was safe. After the press conference, Dr. Wakefield became a marked man.

The Lancet article further awoke the ire of medical industrial complex, and the following month the UK Medical Office of Health convened a conference of selected experts under the auspices of the Medical Research Council to discuss the paper with Wakefield. The Medical Research Council meeting was comprised of 37 experts in virology, epidemiology, gastroenterology, immunology, pediatrics, autism, and child psychiatry. They ostensibly examined published and unpublished "evidence" and concluded that none of the evidence supported the MMR-autism link.

Despite the findings of the Medical Research Council, the fallout from *The Lancet* article was like a hydrogen bomb, and parents in the US and UK started to resist vaccinating their children. The subsequent media storm generated by the press conference and *The Lancet* article produced a seismic backlash from pharmaceutical companies whose profits were threatened and the UK's Department of Health, which feared irrevocable damage to its vaccine programs. Accordingly, the UK uptake of the MMR vaccine had achieved its zenith in 1995 with 95% of children receiving the vaccine, but it plummeted to 81% six years after *The Lancet* article was published. The concerns over the MMR vaccine in the UK were exacerbated when Prime Minister Tony Blair refused to reveal whether or not his son Leo had received an MMR vaccine.

In 2000, Wakefield presented the preliminary results from a study he was conducting to the US Congress. The study's preliminary results showed that tests on 25 children with autism revealed 24 had traces of the measles virus in their gut.

In the wake of Wakefield's appearance before the US Congress, the medical industrial complex intensified its attack against *The Lancet* article. In 2001, the UK's Medical Research Council issued a second report that found no link between the MMR vaccine and autistic spectrum disorders. Moreover, between 2002 and 2004 studies were published in the *British Medical Journal*,[2] *New England Journal of Medicine*,[3] *Pediatrics*,[4] and *The Lancet*[5] maintaining that there wasn't a link between the MMR vaccine and autism.

Although the attacks on Wakefield's research were relentless, the number of children in the UK receiving the MMR vaccine continued to plummet, and *The Lancet* and Wakefield's co-authors continued to support the article. In 2004, however, Wakefield came under the scrutiny of the *Sunday Times*. At the time, the *Sunday Times* was owned by the News Group Newspapers, whose chairman was James Murdoch, the son of Rupert Murdoch.

Paul Nuki was the *Sunday Times'* editor of its "Focus" section, and he commissioned a journalist, Brian Deer, to investigate Wakefield and *The Lancet* article. Although the Murdoch news empire claims to be fair and impartial, it's difficult to discern Paul Nuki approaching the MMR vaccine in a fair and impartial manner, because his father, George Nuki, sat on the UK's Committee on Safety of Medicines, which assesses

2   Taylor B., et al. Measles, mumps, and rubella vaccination and bowel problems or developmental regression in children with autism: population study. BMJ. 2002 Feb 16; 324(7334): 393-6. PMID: 11850369.

3   Madsen K.M., et al. A population-based study of measles, mumps, and rubella vaccination and autism. N Engl J Med. 2002 Nov 7; 347(19): 1477-82. PMID: 12421889.

4   Mäkelä A., Nuorti J.P., Peltola H. Neurological disorders after measles- mumps-rubella vaccination. Pediatrics 2002 Nov 1; 110(5): 957-963. PMID: 12415036.

5   Pichichero M.E., et al. Mercury concentrations and metabolism in infants receiving vaccines containing thimerosal: a descriptive study. Lancet. 2002 Nov 30; 360(9347): 1737-41. PMID: 12480426.

the quality, efficacy and safety of medications, when in 1987 it declared that Smith Kline & French Laboratories' Pluserix MMR vaccine was safe and effective. Smith Kline & French Laboratories eventually morphed into GlaxoSmithKline. Because the UK's Committee on Safety of Medicines found the Pluserix MMR vaccine to be safe and effective, the UK's Joint Committee on Vaccination and Immunization approved the en masse distribution of the Pluserix MMR vaccine in 1988.

Canada withdrew licenses for the Pluserix MMR vaccine in May 1988, because of its deleterious side effects, but the UK's Joint Committee on Vaccination and Immunization nonetheless approved the vaccine following Canada's ban of it. In 1992, however, the Pluserix MMR vaccine was eventually banned in the UK after it was revealed that children developed meningitis after receiving it.

After Paul Nuki commissioned Deer to investigate Wakefield and *The Lancet* article, the latter wrote a series of articles in the *Sunday Times*, starting in February of 2004, pillorying Wakefield and *The Lancet* study. The first article accused Wakefield and his co-authors of not "ethically" recruiting the study's 12 subjects, and it also accused the authors of not receiving a green light from the Royal Free Hospital's ethics committee to perform medical tests on the children. Moreover, the article disclosed that Wakefield had a financial conflict of interest in the study that he didn't disclose to *The Lancet*.

The conflict of interest centered around the fact that Wakefield did not disclose consulting fees he had received from attorneys representing clients who were suing pharmaceutical companies over claims that their children's autism was caused by the MMR vaccine. In fact, eleven of the twelve children in Wakefield's study were part of the litigation.

Wakefield, however, revealed his involvement in the litigation in a letter he sent to *The Lancet* on 2 May 1998, but Deer did not mention this fact in his article. While Deer obsessed about Wakefield 's failure to disclose his involvement in the prospective litigation in his February 1998 article, he ignored the convention at the time that medical scientists rarely disclosed *potential* conflicting interests. Even in the early 2000s, unlike today, it was rare for researchers to disclose potential conflicts of interest in science journals.

Wakefield was also genuinely concerned by his findings, and he thought they should be urgently investigated. I don't believe his stance was anything more than the natural reaction of a concerned clinician who thought there might be a link between the MMR vaccine and autism. He was caught between a rock and a hard place. If he kept quiet about the possible link between the MMR vaccine and autism until the end of possible multi-party litigation that would wend for years, thousands of children might be unnecessarily harmed.

The month after Deer published his initial article on Wakefield, Sir Crispin Davis, the CEO of Reed Elsevier, which owns *The Lancet*, publicly excoriated Wakefield in the House of Commons. Sir Davis neglected to mention in the House of Commons that he had become a non-executive director of MMR manufacturer GlaxoSmithKline the previous month.

After Sir Crispin Davis became a non-executive director of GlaxoSmithKline, his brother, who was a High Court Justice, upheld a decision from a lower court that ruled legal aid should be withdrawn from families who claim their children were damaged vaccines, including GlaxoSmithKline's MMR vaccine. Justice Davis was questioned about a conflict of interest, and in a statement to the press he said, "...the possibility of any conflict of interest arising from his brother's position did not occur to him."

The Lancet conducted a review of Deer's allegations, and, despite Sir Davis' new arrangement with GlaxoSmithKline, the journal concluded that Wakefield and his 12 co-authors hadn't acted unethically, and they, in fact, were given the green light from the Royal Free Hospital's ethics committee to conduct the study. But *The Lancet* concluded that Wakefield did indeed have a financial conflict of interest that he hadn't disclosed to the medical journal when the article was published.

Needless to say, *The Lancet*, Wakefield, and his 12 co-authors had taken extreme heat for the article. Although *The Lancet* found that Wakefield had a conflict of interest that he hadn't disclosed when the article was published, the medical journal still opted not to retract the article. However, ten of Wakefield's co-authors retracted their participation in the article, because they had come to the realization that they were jeopardizing their careers. Like Wakefield, fellow co-authors John Walker-Smith and Simon Murch refused to retract their co-authorship of *The Lancet* article.

Deer followed the initial hatchet job on Wakefield with a second article in November of 2004 that accused Drs. Wakefield and Walker-Smith of applying for a measles vaccine patent on behalf of the Royal Free Hospital medical school and the Neuroimmuno Therapeutics Research Foundation, a private company in Spartanburg, South Carolina. The article contended that Wakefield's vaccine would be a potential competitor to the MMR vaccine and single-shot measles vaccines, so he had financial motivations for his research linking the MMR vaccine to autism.

In 2006, Deer reported on a measles "outbreak" that was occurring in the UK. According to Deer, "The number of confirmed measles cases nationally is already 100 for the first three months of this year, compared with 77 for the whole of 2005." Unfortunately, a 13-year-old boy became the first person in the UK to die from measles in 14 years, and Deer blamed Wakefield for the measles outbreak and for the boy's premature demise.

In an interview with the Autism Awareness Radio Show, Dr. Wakefield responded to the boy's death and his demonization: "The fact that I was being blamed for this epidemic in South Wales, it is bizarre and it is false," he said. "When I made the recommendation of the use of single vaccines in preference to the MMR, then those single vaccines in the U.K., in 1989 and 1988 we're freely available. Single vaccines were freely available on the National Health Services, in other words for free. So parents had a choice of MMR or single vaccines. Six months after I made that recommendation, the government unilaterally withdrew the importation license for the single vaccines. Therefore, making it impossible for parents to get single vaccines on the National Health Service. So removing choice from the parents who may have been genuinely concerned about the safety of the MMR. And as a consequence of that, then the measles came back. That is entirely their fault."

The muckraking of Deer and the *Sunday Times* eventually created the critical mass for the British General Medical Council (GMC) to conduct an inquiry into allegations of misconduct and malfeasance against Drs. Wakefield, John Walker-Smith, and Simon Murch – the three co-authors who refused to retract their participation in *The Lancet* article. The GMC's "inquiry" started in 2007, and the investigation centered on Deer's accusations, which included that children with autism were subjected to unnecessary invasive medical procedures such as colonoscopy and lumbar puncture, and that Wakefield acted without the required ethical approval from the Royal Free Hospital.

The GMC inquiry wended from 2007 to 2010, and it was, by far, the most protracted and costly GMC inquiry in history. As the GMC inquiry was being conducted, journalist Deer started to experience upward mobility, because he began to write for the esteemed *British Journal of Medicine*, which was now remunerating him to deconstruct Wakefield and *The Lancet* article.

Deer had repeatedly accused Wakefield of prevarication, but his attacks on Wakefield in the *British Journal of Medicine* accused Wakefield of falsifying the study's data. As Deer followed the GMC inquiry, he reported in the *British Journal of Medicine* that only one child of the twelve children in The Lancet article were autistic. But, on closer inspection, Deer's reportage in the *British Journal of Medicine*, buttressed by the GMC, was a tissue of lies.

According to Deer, children 1, 4, 5, 6, 7, 8, 12 in the Wakefield et al. study weren't autistic as the authors implied or they had developmental problems before their MMR vaccine, but his reportage contains falsehoods and negates Asperger's as a feature of autism. Deer also assumes that arriving at a diagnosis of autism is straightforward for parents and for doctors, and he simply ignores the often lengthy process that's involved in arriving at an autistic diagnosis. It should also be noted that Deer and the GMC inquiry had access to records and letters from the early 1990s that were not available to Wakefield and his defense team.

For child 1, who received an MMR vaccination at 12 months, Deer and the GMC accused Dr. Wakefield of altering the data of Dr. Walker-Smith's examination of the child demonstrate that the child was autistic. However, the child's general practitioner clearly stated in a letter to Dr. Walker Smith that child 1 was autistic dated May 17, 1996 – after the child's MMR vaccination: "[Child 1] initially developed normally, reaching the normal milestones until he was about 15 months old. He then regressed and has now been diagnosed as autistic."

According to Deer, child 4 had "developmental delays" before he received his MMR vaccination. Deer does not report that child 4 had a measles vaccination at 15 months, prior to his MMR vaccination. Wakefield mentioned this significant fact in *The Lancet* article: "[Child 4] had received monovalent measles vaccine at 15 months, after which his development slowed (confirmed by professional assessors). No association was made with the vaccine at this time. He received a dose of measles, mumps, and rubella vaccine at age 4.5 years, the day after which his mother described a striking deterioration in his behavior that she did link with the immunization." *The Lancet* article referred to both immunizations, noting delayed development after the measles vaccination and a salient delay after the MMR vaccination.

Deer reported that child 5 received an MMR vaccine at 16 months, but the medical records noted parental worries about the child's development at "11 months." The Lancet article doesn't even imply that child 5 was afflicted by autism after an MMR vaccine, so Wakefield can't be accused of lying about child 5. However, three physicians who examined the boy two to five years after he received an MMR vaccination concluded that he had "autism" or "autistic features," but his parents felt that he had developmental delays prior to his MMR vaccination.

Deer wrote that child 6 did not have a diagnosis of autism at "admission or on discharge" from the Royal Free Hospital, but he "had Asperger's syndrome, which is distinct from autism under DSM-IV..." On child 6, Deer displays his ignorance on autism, because Asperger's was considered to be on the spectrum of autistic disorders, but Deer treats the two conditions as unquestionably distinct.

According to Deer, child 7 didn't have an autism diagnosis "either at admission or on discharge from the Royal Free." But Deer fails to mention that the child's general practitioner referred child 7 to a developmental neuro-pediatrician, and the neuro-pediatrician's whose report on child 7 stated the following: "As has been previously suggested, this pattern is that of an autistic disability...his problems are best described as being due to a Pervasive Developmental Disorder in the Autistic Spectrum."

Deer noted that child 8 had congenital "coarctation of the aorta," which has the potential to cause developmental delays. He wrote that a report from her consulting pediatrician said that her "coarctation" occurred "side by side" with her developmental "delay."

For child 8, Deer is reporting an outright falsehood, because in the report that Deer referred to that is dated May 1994, child 8's consulting pediatrician stated: "My impression was that she is a child who is developing within normal limits, but in whom I thought I may have found congenital heart disease as an incidental finding." Deer's quote refers to an examination that raised developmental concerns shortly after child received an MMR vaccine – after her aorta had been surgically repaired. Her consulting physician wrote the following about child 8 when he examined her on February 17, 1995 – within a month of receiving an MMR vaccination: "She was recently admitted to the ward [on 13 February 1995] following a febrile convulsion in association with gastroenteritis.... There were no neurological abnormalities other than the developmental delay."

Deer noted that child 12 had Asperger's syndrome, and, as with child 6, he displayed his ignorance concerning autistic disorders due to the fact that Asperger's syndrome falls into the spectrum of autistic disorders.

In addition to accusing Wakefield of being deceptive, and also of having undisclosed conflicts of interest, the GMC accused Drs. Wakefield, Walker-Smith, and Murch of conducting procedures, such as colonoscopies, colon biopsies, and "spinal taps" without the approval of the department's ethics board and contrary to the children's clinical interests, because they were not indicated by the children's symptoms or medical history. But Drs. Wakefield, Walker-Smith, and Murch argued that the procedures were clinically indicated due to the children's gastroenterological problems.

As the GMC was in the homestretch of its deliberations on the fates of Drs. Wakefield, Walker-Smith, and Murch, and the *Sunday Times* continued its unabated attacks on the besieged physicians, James Murdoch was appointed a non-executive director of GlaxoSmithKline.

On January 28, 2010, after hearing evidence for nearly three years, the five-member GMC tribunal found Drs. Wakefield, Walker-Smith, and Murch guilty of multiple counts of misconduct and ethical violations. The media, particularly the *Sunday Times* and *British Journal of Medicine*, trumpeted the GMC verdict with glee. The Lancet also categorically retracted their 1998 article.

Later in 2010, Drs. Wakefield and Walker-Smith were stripped of their medical degrees and banned from practicing medicine. Although the GMC tribunal declared that Dr. Murch was guilty of multiple counts of misconduct, it concluded that Dr. Murch demonstrated errors of judgment, but he had acted in good faith and that any professional misconduct on his part, such as performing colonoscopies that were not clinically indicated didn't reach the threshold of serious professional misconduct, because he was following the directions of Dr. Walker-Smith, his superior.

Dr. Walker-Smith had malpractice insurance that funded the expenses he accrued appealing the GMC verdict, but Dr. Wakefield was left financially devastated and his malpractice insurance wasn't obligated to finance his appeal of the GMC verdict. In March of 2012, Dr. Walker-Smith was exonerated by the UK's High Court. Justice John Mitting ruled that the conclusions of GMC were based on "inadequate and superficial reasoning and, in a number of instances, a wrong conclusion."

The verdict restored Walker-Smith's name to the medical register and his reputation to the medical community. For advocates of autistic children who have been harmed by vaccines the High Court's ruling wasn't surprising, because the GMC trial had no actual complainants from patients, no harm came to the children who were studied, and parents supported Wakefield and Walker-Smith through the trial, reporting that their children had medically benefited from the treatment they received at the Royal Free Hospital. Indeed, all of the complaints against Drs. Wakefield, Walker-Smith, and Murch found their genesis in the reportage of Brian Deer.

After Dr. Wakefield was stripped of his license to practice medicine, he moved to the US, where he established The Johnson Center for Child Health and Development, which is based in Austin, Texas. The objective of The Johnson Center is to gain a better understanding of childhood developmental disorders through clinical care, research and education.

Dr. Wakefield realized that if launched a defamation lawsuit against Brian Deer and British Journal of Medicine in the UK, he wouldn't have a snowball's chance in hell, so he filed a defamation lawsuit against Brian Deer and the *British Journal of Medicine* in a Texas court. The presiding judge, however, quashed the lawsuit because of jurisdictional issues, ruling that Dr. Wakefield didn't have the right to sue any of the parties involved as they are outside the US, and Texas' Third Court of Appeals held up the judge's ruling.

Although the medical industrial complex and the media have demonized Dr. Wakefield for his belief that the MMR vaccine is linked to autism, the actual efficacy of the MMR vaccine has been overlooked. A 2008 article in the *New England Journal of Medicine* reported on a mumps outbreak in the US in 2006. [6]A total of 6,584 cases of mumps were reported that year. For the 12 years preceding the outbreak, the national coverage of one-dose of the MMR vaccine among preschoolers was 89%, and it was 86% or more in highly affected states.

6   Dayan G.H., et al. Recent resurgence of mumps in the United States. N Engl J Med 2008 Apr 10: 358(15): 1580-9. PMID: 18403766.

Chapter Eleven

An Absolute Disaster

In 2012, the House's Committee on Oversight and Government Reform held a hearing on the rising incidence of autism entitled "1 In 88 Children: A Look into the Federal Response to Rising Rates of Autism." Eight years had lapsed since the Committee on Oversight and Government Reform's last hearing on autism, even though the epidemic was growing considerably more detrimental with each passing year.

In 2004 the Committee on Oversight and Government Reform held a hearing entitled, "Truth Revealed: New Scientific Discoveries Regarding Mercury in Medicine and Autism." Since the 2012 hearing on autism held in November of 2012, and February of 2015, the House has held 135 hearings. 25 hearings were focused on government waste and mismanagement, 20 hearings pertained to the IRS, 20 other hearings brought "Obama Care" into the limelight, and four centered around marijuana. Spare one Subcommittee for ASD. Unfortunately, autism had become a low priority for Congress.

Despite this fact, however, a number of onlookers and people who had been personally affected by autism welcomed the 2012 hearing, because so many events had transpired in the arena of autism over the preceding eight years. The previous eight years had seen the unimpeded growth of autism, the rise and fall of the Geiers, the public crucifixion of Dr. Wakefield, Dr. Thorsen was still a fugitive from justice, etc.

The chairpersonship of the House's Committee on Oversight and Government Reform has a six-year term limit, so Dan Burton had to relinquish his chairmanship of the Committee in 2003, but he remained on the Committee as a member. Although Burton had most likely sparked ire and fear in the hearts of the CDC, FDA, and Big Pharma, he was ultimately unable to significantly dent their monolith of lies and deception.

U.S. Representative Darrell Issa, a Republican from California, became the chairperson of the Committee on Oversight and Government Reform in 2011, so he chaired the 2012 hearing – "1 In 88 Children: A Look into the Federal Response to Rising Rates of Autism." Unlike Congressman Burton, Congressman Issa had received a substantial largesse from Big Pharma in the form of campaign contributions – approximately $300,000. He obviously didn't feel compelled to bite the hand that fed him, and the 2012 hearing was choreographed to obfuscate the truth.

Representative Issa called Dr. Alan Guttmacher, Director of the Eunice Kennedy Shriver National Institute of Child Health and Human Development, National Institutes of Health, as the Committee's first witness. Dr. Guttmacher's opening remarks pertained to the good works of the *Interagency Autism Coordinating Committee* (IACC), which coordinates all efforts within the Department of Health and Human Services concerning autism that encompasses activities carried out through the NIH and the CDC. Under the Combating Autism Act that was signed into law in December of 2006 by President George W. Bush, the IACC is a public/private hybrid agency that includes at least one-third public members, a person with autism, and a person who is the parent of a child with autism.

The IACC sounds like a superlative idea in theory, because it incorporates individuals who aren't government apparatchiks and also victims of autism's blight. But, unfortunately, like most of government machinations pertaining to autism, if people scratch below the surface, they will encounter the perfidious.

Thomas Insel is the Chairperson of the IACC, and he is also the Director of the National Institute of Mental Health (NIMH), the component of the NIH charged with generating the knowledge needed to understand, treat, and prevent mental disorders. The NIH, like the CDC, is in the business of promoting vaccinations. However, the conflict of interest doesn't stop with Thomas Insel being employed by an organization who's in the business of promoting vaccinations. Thomas Insel's brother, Richard A. Insel, was the co-founder and director of Praxis-Biologics, a vaccine development company in Rochester, N.Y., which developed the HibTITER, an influenza vaccine. Praxis-Biologics was sold to Cyanamid, an American conglomerate, in a deal valued at $190 million, which netted Richard A. Insel close to $4 million. It should also be noted that the Hib influenza vaccine is in our recommended immunization schedule, and Pfizer largely gobbled Cyanamid up in 2009.

After Dr. Guttmacher spoke of the IACC's good works, and neglected to mention that IACC Chairperson Insel had gaping conflicts of interest, Dr. Coleen Boyle of the CDC was called before the Committee. Dr. Boyle, the beacon of veracity who we've met before, was now the Director of the National Center on Birth Defects and Developmental Disabilities – instead of the Acting Director – demonstrating that perjuring herself before Congress correlated with upward mobility at the CDC.

Dr. Boyle's statement elucidated the CDC's due diligence concerning autism. She discussed the CDC's "supporting communities" by tracking ASD, helping families "through early intervention," and, of course, the CDC's cutting edge research into the cause of autism. Dr. Boyle never mentioned the word vaccine in her statement to the Committee.

Chairperson Issa was the first Committee member to ply questions to Dr. Guttmacher and Dr. Boyle, and they were mere softballs. Representative Cummings, who was the Committee's ranking Democrat, was the second Committee member to pose questions to Dr. Guttmacher and Dr. Boyle, and he too lobbed softballs.

The third member of the Committee to question Dr. Guttmacher and Dr. Boyle was Representative Dan Burton, who was allotted five minutes for questions. Representative

Burton showed a two-minute video that was made by the University of Calgary's Department of Physiology and Biophysics that demonstrated the extremely destructive properties of mercury on human brain neurons. After the video was shown to the Committee, Representative Burton only had three minutes to ask questions to Dr. Guttmacher and Dr. Boyle, but he wasn't lobbing softballs. Indeed, he embarked on a tirade of exasperation:

> Now, we've gone from 1 in 10,000 children known to be autistic to 1 in 88. It is worse than an epidemic; it is an absolute disaster. And how anybody can look at that study and see the actual brain cells deteriorating when put next to a very small, minute amount of mercury, it mystifies me. How can anybody at the CDC and the FDA watch something like that and say that the mercury does not have an impact on neurological problems? Now, granted, it may be from other things besides vaccinations, but vaccinations that contain mercury should not under any circumstances be injected into any human being, especially children, who have a very fragile immune system. And children get as many as 28 or 30 shots before they go to the first grade. My grandson got nine shots in 1 day, and it turned him into a horrible situation that we found banging his head against the wall, couldn't go to the bathroom, all kinds of things. These people won't tell you all about that. So all I would – I would pray to you, beg you to go back to FDA and HHS and say, come on, let's get with it. There may be other causes, but let's get mercury out of all vaccinations, which is a contributing factor. If you do that, and you can go to single-shot vials, it costs, what, a penny, 2 cents apiece, it won't hurt anything. And I don't mind if the pharmaceutical companies get legislation passed here that protects them from class-action lawsuits as long as they help the Vaccine Injury Compensation Fund and get mercury out of these vaccinations.

Representative Burton's soliloquy was impassioned, because he was retiring from the House of Representatives after 30 years. Over the preceding years he had amassed considerable power in Congress, but he was still unable to force the CDC to come clean about vaccines. So he made one final plea for the CDC and NIH to correct a grave injustice: "I'm leaving. I'm not going to be here anymore. You won't have to watch me up here anymore. But please go back and work on it, will you?"

After Representative Burton's plea to the CDC and NIH, the Committee members continued to lob softballs at Dr. Guttmacher and Dr. Boyle – until it came to Dennis Kucinich, a Democratic Representative from Ohio. Representative Kucinich cited a study that was conducted by researchers at the University of Texas who found that there was a significant increase in the rates of special education students and autism associated with increases in environmentally released mercury from coal fired power plants.[1] Dr. Guttmacher, the NIH expert, wasn't aware of the study; Dr. Boyle said she was aware of the study, but it was unique, because it analyzed such a vast population.

The members of the Committee continued to lob softballs at Dr. Guttmacher and Dr. Boyle until it rolled around to Bill Posey, a Republican from Florida. Posey wasn't a member of the Committee, but he asked to sit in on the hearing. Posey had taken over the representation of the eighth district of Florida after Dave Weldon had relinquished it. Posey was a friend of Weldon, and Weldon had told him about the CDC malfeasance regarding vaccines, so he was eager to ply Dr. Boyle with questions.

Representative Posey commenced his allotted five minutes, citing an article he read that said autism in Africa was non-existent until Westerners introduced vaccines to the continent, and he wondered if the CDC had conducted or facilitated a study that compared autism rates between vaccinated and unvaccinated children. Dr. Boyle attempted to muddy the waters by discussing studies that weren't germane to Representative Posey's question. Finally, Posey cut her off and said, "My time is very limited here. So, clearly, definitely, unequivocally you have studied vaccinated ver-

1   Palmer R.F., Blanchard S., Wood R. Proximity to point sources of environmental mercury release as a predictor of autism prevalence. Health Place. 2009 March; 15(1): 18-24. PMID: 18353703.

sus unvaccinated?" And Dr. Boyle responded: "We have not studied vaccinated versus unvaccinated."

After Representative Posey told Dr. Boyle that she had wasted two minutes of his time with her circumlocution, he asked if the integrity of the Thorson studies had been validated. He referred to Thorson as "one of the most wanted men on Earth." Dr. Boyle responded that Thorson was merely responsible for two studies that didn't link thimerosal to autism, and she said that the "body of work" demonstrates there's no correlation between thimerosal and autism is a "large collection of studies."

"I have seen a chart that ranks the longevity of the 30 nations with the best mortality rates in the world, starting with Iceland, Sweden, Singapore and on down. We didn't even make the top 30," said Representative Posey. "We are the 34th. And ironically, we require more vaccinations than any other country that is healthier and has a less mortality rate than us. Do you see any correlation whatsoever, either one of you, to the 34th worst mortality rate and the most vaccinations to the ones with the least required vaccinations and the lowest mortality rate?"

Dr. Guttmacher's response to Representative Posey equated the longevity in the United States to vaccinations, and Representative Posey replied that he wasn't against vaccines, but, rather, he was against a "bomb blast of vaccines" with thimerosal. Just as Representative Posey commented on the "bomb blast of vaccines" with thimerosal that had been forced into the bodies of American children, his allotted five minutes expired. Dr. Guttmacher was asked if he wanted to respond to Representative Posey's comment, and he replied: "No, thank you."

After Representative Posey's aggressive questioning of Dr. Guttmacher and Dr. Boyle, the questions posed by the subsequent Committee members were, for the most part, benign, and Dr. Guttmacher and Dr. Boyle glided through them – with the exception of the questions asked by Representative Carolyn Maloney, a Democrat from New York. "I must have had 50 different parents write me or come to me and say, I had a healthy child, yet then they have 10, 9, 6 vaccinations at one time, and that child changed overnight and was knocking their head on the wall, and it was a changed child," said Representative Maloney. "In fact, I had a family in my office today where the mother broke down crying, saying, 'My child was wonderful, bright, precocious, talking. She took those vaccinations, and the child became very incredibly sick and has never recovered.' So I'm interested in any studies on vaccinations and trying to understand that. Now, it used to be that you'd go and get a vaccination. My child never got more than three at a time. And in the State of New York, children are recommended to get six shots every 2 months throughout the first year of a child. And my question is, why does the schedule of these vaccines – vaccinations require a child to receive so many shots in such a short period of time?"

Dr. Boyle replied to Representative Maloney's query with the CDC's standard response: "There is a Federal advisory committee that determines the vaccination schedule. And the reason – and, again, I'll – we'll clarify this and get you more information, but the reason – the reason they cluster the vaccines is really to try to make sure that everyone gets it. People don't – and again, we're trying to make sure vaccines go to all children. And not everybody goes to the doctor routinely, so they use – they use that opportunity to make sure that happens."

Representative Vern Buchanan, a Republican from Florida, followed Representative Maloney, and he piggybacked on Representative Maloney's line of questioning: "Is it true that we have over 40 vaccines? And I'm not against vaccines, all of them, either. But let me just say, because I know there's a lot of evidence that they're good, but don't we get, like, 40-some vaccines, our children, today? Is that the number? I'm hearing upward of 40?

Dr. Guttmacher didn't reply with a specific number of vaccinations that are forced on children, but he said that "40 is a little bit high." In reality, however, 40 isn't a bit high. An American child receives 49 doses of 14 vaccines before the age 6, and 69 doses of 16 vaccines by age 18.

Representative Posey was allowed an additional question after the members of the Committee had questioned Dr.

Guttmacher and Dr. Boyle, and he didn't pose a question to Dr. Guttmacher and Dr. Boyle. Instead, he pointed out that Dr. Thorson wasn't involved in "two studies" as Dr. Boyle had testified; he was actually involved in 21 studies that the invalidated a link between thimerosal and autism. Dr. Boyle had perjured herself before Congress with impunity yet again.

After the Committee members questioned Dr. Guttmacher and Dr. Boyle, the Committee called the following six individuals who were affiliated with various private organizations that were dedicated to addressing the problems and issues surrounding ASD:

- Mr. Bob Wright, Co-Founder, Autism Speaks

- Mr. Scott Badesch, President, Autism Society

- Mr. Mark Blaxill, Board Member, Safeminds

- Mr. Bradley McGarry, Coordinator of the Asperger Initiative at Mercyhurst University

- Mr. Michael John Carley, Executive Director, Global & Regional Asperger Syndrome Partnership

- Mr. Ari Ne'eman, President, Autistic Self Advocacy Network

Of the six individuals called to testify before the Committee, only Mark Blaxill of Safeminds discussed the link between thimerosal and autism and also the malfeasance of the CDC. In fact, Scott Badesch, President of the Autism Society, had publicly stated that there was a "zero" correlation between vaccines and autism. Blaxill had a daughter who was autistic, so he had personally felt the blight of autism.

"I think we have to face reality," said Blaxill. "We need to be clear: Autism is a public health crisis of historic proportions, worse than poliomyelitis. It's devastating a generation of children and their families. We need to face that reality. Autism is a national emergency."

Blaxill's PowerPoint presentation before the Committee expounded on the CDC's manipulation of autism rates at

Brick, New Jersey and the manipulation of autism rates on the Verstraeten study.

"I'll just say that in the financial world, the result of pressure to manipulate numbers to provide the answers that bosses want has a name; it's called securities fraud. In medicine there are similar pressures; they are called special-interest politics and even peer review," Blaxill told the Committee. "And what the CDC has given us is the medical equivalent of securities fraud all to avoid the inconvenient reality of the autism epidemic. In the face of a national emergency, government agencies, especially CDC and NIH, have performed poorly and behaved badly. We need accountable, new leadership on autism at NIH and CDC. We need an advisory committee that believes in combating autism, not newly stocked with – one newly stocked with appointees who actually oppose that mission. We need a Combating Autism Act that truly combats autism. We need to stop investing in the autism gene hunt and identify what has changed in the environment that could possibly have injured so many children. The scope and the magnitude of these changes, it's complicated, yes, but it can't be that complicated. There has to be a very small list of things that could have changed."

Many of the Committee members shied away from asking Blaxill questions, but Blaxill's comments about Brick, New Jersey piqued the interest of Representative Chris Smith, a Republican from New Jersey. Representative Smith had seen the CDC's and the Agency for Toxic Substances and Disease Registry's whitewash of the epidemic of autism that descended on Brick, New Jersey, and he actually thought those government agencies were telling the truth, when they stated that there wasn't an autism epidemic in Brick Township. He asked Blaxill what motives scientists had for covering up such matters.

"...we are in contact with scientists. And the private conversations you have with scientists is that there are third rails. There are politically incorrect issues," Blaxill replied. "There is – there are career consequences for doing a certain kind of study, and there have been ritual punishments of certain scientists out there, some very public, some more private, and there are innumerable, there are many examples of those. That is – and when the scientists say, oh, we should let the scientists take care of that, no. It is not a self-regulating process because, in fact, the leaders of NIH enforce the orthodoxy of the scientific establishment, and if you take on third rail questions, those are suppressed. We have many examples of those. I could provide some more."

Despite the efforts of Congressmen Burton and Posey and some of the other Committee members, the House's Committee on Oversight and Government Reform "1 In 88 Children: A Look into the Federal Response to Rising Rates of Autism" hearing ended up in a stalemate. The hearing didn't compel the CDC or NIH to come clean, and, once more, a Committee on Oversight and Government Reform autism hearing accomplished nothing. Chairman Issa said that the "1 In 88 Children: A Look into the Federal Response to Rising Rates of Autism" hearing would be followed by another hearing on autism if necessary. In fact, there was another hearing in May of 2014, "Examining the Federal Response to Autism Spectrum Disorders." which succumbed to the inauspicious nature of a smaller-shorter subcommittee hearing. It never received the same ballyhooed media coverage as the first one. I didn't even know there was a second hearing until doing research for this book.

However, as observed by Subcommittee Chair John Mica (R-Fla), the CDC's new autism prevalence rate was now 1:68 compared to 1:88. Which represents a 33 percent increase from the previous year. Additionally, two studies[2] cited by Congressman Posey clearly demonstrated that there was a much greater environmental factor involved, for children developing autism than previously thought.

---

2   Sven Sandin MSc., et al. The familia risk of autism. JAMA. 2014; 311(17): 1770-1777, and;

Hallmayer J., et al. Genetic heritability and shared environmental factorsamong twin pairs with autism. Arch Gen Psychiatry. 2011 Nov; 68(11): 1095-102. PMID: 21727249.

CHAPTER TWELVE

THE INCREDIBLE SHRINKING ASD

As I mentioned in Chapter 1, according to a 2014 study by the CDC, 1 in 68 American children have a diagnosis that falls into *"autism spectrum disorder"* or *ASD* in 2010. Many people dismiss the severity of this epidemic as they falsely believe the diagnosis of autism has been broadened, therefore more people are being diagnosed as autistic, which was a point made by Dr. Boyle during her testimony at the "1 In 88 Children: A Look into the Federal Response to Rising Rates of Autism." But the beliefs of Dr. Boyle and other people who contend that the broadening the diagnosis of autism is partially responsible for its unimpeded growth aren't grounded in reality, because the diagnosis of autism has been actually constricted in recent years.

Autism was first described in a 1943 paper "Autistic Disturbances of Affective Contact," authored by Leo Kanner, MD, a psychiatrist at Johns Hopkins University, who founded the first child psychiatry clinic in the country.[1] Dr. Kanner's groundbreaking 1943 paper described eleven children who shared high intelligence, a profound preference for being alone and an "obsessive insistence on the preservation of sameness." These eleven children perplexed Dr. Kanner, because he had never encountered their pathology.

The seventh case of autism diagnosed by Dr. Kanner was John Trevett, who was called "Herbert B." in Kanner's 1943

---

1   Kanner l. Autistic disturbances of affective contact. Nerv Child, 2: 217-50. Reprint, Acta Paedopsychiatr. 1968; 35(4): 100-36. PMID 4880460.

paper. Interestingly, John Trevett's mother was Elizabeth Peabody Trevett, a pediatrician and a pioneer in the promotion of mass vaccinations for infants. She presumably vaccinated her baby, and perhaps herself while pregnant, with the same shots that she administered to her own patients, and one of the vaccines was the newly developed diphtheria toxoid, which was the first vaccine to contain thimerosal.

Among the initial 11 patients Dr. Kanner diagnosed with autism were children whose parents were heavily exposed to mercury. One parent was a plant pathologist experimenting with ethylmercury fungicides in Maryland, and another parent was a stenographer in a pathology lab in Washington, D.C., who spent her workday exposed to mercury fumes.

Throughout the 1960s, psychiatrists continued to view autism as a form of "childhood schizophrenia." Autism was also thought to be the resultant effect of emotionally distant mothering. The 1970s brought a new understanding that autism stemmed from biological differences in brain development, and objective criteria for diagnosing autism followed in the 1980s.

The current diagnosis criteria of ASD is a long and winding road that begins and ends with the *Diagnostic and Statistical Manual: Mental Disorders (DSM)*, which is the "Bible" by which mental health professionals make diagnoses. Prior to the DSM, the International Statistical Classification of Diseases and Related Health Problems, usually termed the International Classification of Diseases (ICD), was the international "standard diagnostic tool for epidemiology, health management and clinical purposes."

The ICD finds it origins in the latter half of the 1800s, but in 1946 it came under the purview of the World Health Organization, which is the directing and coordinating authority for health within the United Nations. The World Health Organization regularly updates the ICD, and in 1994 the 10th (ICD-10) edition was published. The 11th edition (ICD-11) is due in 2017.

The American Psychiatric Association Committee on Nomenclature and Statistics developed a variant of the ICD-6 that was published in 1952 as the first edition of *Di-*

agnostic and Statistical Manual: Mental Disorders (DSM-I). The DSM-I contained a glossary of descriptions for various diagnostic categories and was the first official manual of mental disorders to focus on clinical utility. The DSM, like the ICD, is regularly updated.

Autism was so rare that the term was absent from the initial two editions of the DSM and also from the initial seven editions of the ICD. In 1980, the 3rd edition of the DSM (DSM III) was published, and it introduced the diagnosis Infantile Autism, which had the following six features:

1.Onset before 30 months of age

2. Pervasive lack of responsiveness to other people

3. Gross deficits in language development

4. If speech is present, peculiar speech patterns such as immediate and delayed echolalia, metaphorical language, pronominal reversal

5. Bizarre responses to various aspects of the environment, e.g., resistance to change, peculiar interest in or attachments to animate or inanimate objects

6. Absence of delusions, hallucinations, loosening of associations, and incoherence as in schizophrenia.

The DSM-IV was published in 1994, and it had the most inclusive diagnosis of ASD, because as an umbrella term for ASD the DSM-VI included Autistic Disorder, Pervasive Developmental Disorder, Not Otherwise Specified (PDD-NOS), Asperger's Disorder, Rett's Disorder, and Childhood Disintegrative Disorder. The following are the DSM-IV classifications for ASD:

AUTISTIC DISORDER

A total of six symptoms from categories 1, 2, 3, with at least two symptoms from category 1, and one each from categories 2 and 3:

1. Qualitative impairment in social interaction, as manifested by at least two of the following:

• Marked impairment in the use of multiple nonverbal behaviors, such as eye-to-eye gaze, facial expression, body postures, and gestures to regulate social interaction, failure to develop peer relationships appropriate to developmental level

• A lack of spontaneous seeking to share enjoyment, interests, or achievements with other people (e.g., by a lack of showing, bringing, or pointing out objects of interest)

• A lack of social or emotional reciprocity

2. Qualitative impairments in communication, as manifested by at least one of the following:

• Delay in, or total lack of, the development of spoken language (not accompanied by an attempt to compensate through alternative modes of communication such as gesture or mime)

• In individuals with adequate speech, marked impairment in the ability to initiate or sustain a conversation with others

• Stereotyped and repetitive use of language or idiosyncratic language

• A lack of varied, spontaneous make-believe play or social imitative play appropriate to developmental level

3. Restricted, repetitive, and stereotyped patterns of behavior, interests, and activities as manifested by at least one of the following:

• Encompassing preoccupation with one or more stereotyped and restricted patterns of interest that is abnormal either in intensity or focus

• Apparently inflexible adherence to specific, nonfunctional routines or rituals

• Stereotyped and repetitive motor mannerisms (e.g., hand or finger flapping or twisting or complex whole-body movements)

• Persistent preoccupation with parts of objects

111

4. Delays or abnormal functioning in at least one of the following areas, with onset prior to age 3 years:

• social interaction,

• language as used in social communication, or

• symbolic or imaginative play.

5. The disturbance is not better accounted for by Rett's disorder or childhood disintegrative disorder.

PERVASIVE DEVELOPMENTAL DISORDER, NOT OTHERWISE SPECIFIED

Severe and pervasive impairment in the development of reciprocal social interaction or verbal and nonverbal communication skills, or when stereotyped behavior, interests, and activities are present, but the criteria are not met for a specific pervasive developmental disorder, schizophrenia, schizotypal personality disorder, or avoidant personality disorder. For example, this category includes "atypical autism" – presentations that do not meet the criteria for autistic disorder because of late age of onset, atypical symptomatology, or subthreshold symptomatology, or all of these.

ASPERGER'S DISORDER

1. A qualitative impairment in social interaction, as manifested by at least two of the following:

• Marked impairment in the use of multiple nonverbal behaviors, such as eye-to-eye gaze, facial expression, body postures, and gestures to regulate social interaction

• Failure to develop peer relationships appropriate to developmental level

• A lack of spontaneous seeking to share enjoyment, interests, or achievements with other people (e.g., by a lack of showing, bringing, or pointing out objects of interest to other people)

• A lack of social or emotional reciprocity

2. Restricted, repetitive, and stereotyped patterns of behavior, interests, and activities, as manifested by at least one of the following:

> • Encompassing preoccupation with one or more stereotyped and restricted patterns of interest that is abnormal either in intensity or focus

> • Apparently inflexible adherence to specific, nonfunctional routines or rituals

> • Stereotyped and repetitive motor mannerisms (e.g., hand or finger flapping or twisting, or complex whole-body movements)

> • A persistent preoccupation with parts of objects

3. The disturbance causes clinically significant impairment in social, occupational, or other important areas of functioning.

4. There is no clinically significant general delay in language (e.g., single words used by age 2 years, communicative phrases used by age 3 years).

5. There is no clinically significant delay in cognitive development or in the development of age-appropriate self-help skills, adaptive behavior (other than in social interaction), and curiosity about the environment in childhood.

6. Criteria are not met for another specific pervasive developmental disorder or schizophrenia.

Rett's Disorder

1. Apparently normal prenatal and perinatal development

2. Apparently normal psychomotor development through the first five months after birth

3. Normal head circumference at birth

4. Onset of all of the following after the period of normal development:

> • Deceleration of head growth between ages 5 and 48 months

113

• Loss of previously acquired purposeful hand skills between ages 5 and 30 months with the subsequent development of stereotyped hand movements (i.e., hand-wringing or hand washing)

• Loss of social engagement early in the course (although often social interaction develops later)

• Appearance of poorly coordinated gait or trunk movements

• Severely impaired expressive and receptive language development with severe psychomotor retardation

CHILDHOOD DISINTEGRATIVE DISORDER

1. Apparently normal development for at least the first 2 years after birth as manifested by the presence of age-appropriate verbal and nonverbal communication, social relationships, play, and adaptive behavior. But clinically significant loss of previously acquired skills (before age 10 years) in at least two of the following areas:

• Expressive or receptive language

• Social skills or adaptive behavior

• Bowel or bladder control

• Play

• Motor skills

2. Abnormalities of functioning in at least two of the following areas:

• Qualitative impairment in social interaction (e.g., impairment in nonverbal behaviors, failure to develop peer relationships, lack of social or emotional reciprocity)

• Qualitative impairments in communication (e.g., delay or lack of spoken language, inability to initiate or sustain a conversation, stereotyped and repetitive use of language, lack of varied make-believe play)

• Restricted, repetitive, and stereotyped patterns of behavior, interests, and activities, including motor stereotypies and mannerisms

3. The disturbance is not better accounted for by another specific pervasive developmental disorder or by schizophrenia.

The American Psychiatric Association published the DSM-IV Text Revision (DSM-IV-TR) in 2000, and it severely restricted the definition of ASD by removing Rett's Disorder and Childhood Disintegrative Disorder from the developmental disorders that constitute ASD. Despite ablating Rett's Disorder and Childhood Disintegrative Disorder from the DSM-IV-TR, the rate of ASD continued to proliferate.

A 2014 study conducted by the CDC that analyzed the prevalence of ASD in 2010 used the more stringent DSM-IV-TR criteria for ASD and found that 1 in 68 American children suffered from ASD. The 2010 prevalence of ASD was roughly 30% higher than the estimate for 2008 (1 in 88), 60% higher than the estimate for 2006 (1 in 110), and 120% higher than the estimates for 2000 and 2002 (1 in 150). So contrary to popular belief, the definition of ASD has been constricted, but yet the rates of ASD continue to proliferate exponentially.

Throughout the course of this book, I've delineated numerous miscarriages of justice regarding autism, but 2013 proved to be a particularly harsh year for children with autism, their parents, and their advocates, because the DSM-V, published in 2013, severely constricted the diagnosis of ASD. For starters, the DSM-V removed Asperger syndrome and pervasive developmental disorder-not otherwise specified from its classification for ASD. Moreover, the DSM-V requires more total symptoms to be met in the areas of social/communication deficits and repetitive/restrictive behaviors than did the DSM-IV-TR. The following constitutes the DSM-V's criteria for the diagnosis of ASD:

Autism Spectrum Disorder
Must meet all three behavioral criteria in category 1, and at least two in category 2.

1. Persistent deficits in social communication and social interaction across contexts, not accounted for by general developmental delays, and manifest by all 3 of the following:

• Deficits in social-emotional reciprocity; ranging from abnormal social approach and failure of normal back and forth conversation through reduced sharing of interests, emotions, and affect and response to total lack of initiation of social interaction.

• Deficits in nonverbal communicative behaviors used for social interaction; ranging from poorly integrated-verbal and nonverbal communication, through abnormalities in eye contact and body-language, or deficits in understanding and use of nonverbal communication, to total lack of facial expression or gestures.

• Deficits in developing and maintaining relationships, appropriate to developmental level (beyond those with caregivers); ranging from difficulties adjusting behavior to suit different social contexts through difficulties in sharing imaginative play and in making friends, to an apparent absence of interest in people

2. Restricted, repetitive patterns of behavior, interests, or activities as manifested by at least two of the following:

• Stereotyped or repetitive speech, motor movements, or use of objects; (such as simple motor stereotypies, echolalia, repetitive use of objects, or idiosyncratic phrases).

• Excessive adherence to routines, ritualized patterns of verbal or nonverbal behavior, or excessive resistance to change; (such as motoric rituals, insistence on same route or food, repetitive questioning or extreme distress at small changes).

• Highly restricted, fixated interests that are abnormal in intensity or focus; (such as strong attachment to or preoccupation with unusual objects, excessively circumscribed or perseverative interests).

• Hyper-or hypo-reactivity to sensory input or unusual interest in sensory aspects of environment; (such as apparent indifference to pain/heat/cold, adverse response to specific sounds or textures, excessive smelling or touching of objects, fascination with lights or spinning objects).

Symptoms must be present in early childhood (but may not become fully manifest until social demands exceed limited capacities)

Symptoms together limit and impair everyday functioning. There are also 3 new "Severity Levels" for ASD.

LEVEL 3: 'REQUIRING VERY SUBSTANTIAL SUPPORT'

Severe deficits in verbal and nonverbal social communication skills cause severe impairments in functioning; very limited initiation of social interactions and minimal response to social overtures from others.

Preoccupations, fixated rituals and/or repetitive behaviors markedly interfere with functioning in all spheres. Marked distress when rituals or routines are interrupted; very difficult to redirect from fixated interest or returns to it quickly.

LEVEL 2: 'REQUIRING SUBSTANTIAL SUPPORT'

Marked deficits in verbal and nonverbal social communication skills; social impairments apparent even with supports in place; limited initiation of social interactions and reduced or abnormal response to social overtures from others.

RRBs (Rituals and repetitive behaviors) and/or preoccupations or fixated interests appear frequently enough to be obvious to the casual observer and interfere with functioning in a variety of contexts. Distress or frustration is apparent when RRB's are interrupted; difficult to redirect from fixated interest.

LEVEL 1: 'REQUIRING SUPPORT'

Without supports in place, deficits in social communication cause noticeable impairments. Has difficulty initiating social interactions and demonstrates clear examples of atypical or unsuccessful responses to social overtures of others. May appear to have decreased interest in social interactions.

RRB's cause significant interference with functioning in one or more contexts. Resists attempts by others to interrupt RRB's or to be redirected from fixated interest.

Several studies have scrutinized the DSM-V criteria for ASD, and those studies have concluded that the new criteria will eliminate tens of thousands of children from being diagnosed with ASD, which will deprive them of various services that they desperately require.

A 2012 study published in the *Journal of the American Academy of Child and Adolescent Psychiatry* analyzed the records of 657 individuals with ASD, whose ages ranged from 12 months to 43 years old, who participated in the clinical trials for the DSM-IV, and it re-evaluated those individuals using the DSM-5 criteria.[2] The researchers found that 39.4% of the individuals would no longer qualify for a diagnosis of ASD. By diagnosis, the new criteria excluded 24.2% of those with Autistic Disorder, 75% of those with Asperger's disorder, and 71.7% of those with PDD-NOS.

A 2012 study published in *Developmental Neurorehabilitation* screened a population of 2,721 toddlers (age 17-36 months) at risk for a developmental disability.[3] The researchers concluded that, potentially, there could be a 47.79% decrease in diagnosis of ASD as a result of the diagnostic criteria proposed by the DSM-V. The children who met criteria for PDD-NOS were disproportionately impacted, because 79.94% of them did not meet the proposed DSM-5 criteria for ASD.

Dr. Susan Swedo, chair of the Neurodevelopmental Disorders Workgroup for the DSM-5, which spearheaded the criteria change for ASD in the DSM-V, presented the results of the DSM-V field trials for autism to the Interagency Au-

2   McPartland J.C., Reichow B., Volkmar F.R. Sensitivity and specificity of proposed DSM-5 diagnostic criteria for autism spectrum disorder. J Am Acad Child Adolesc Psychiatry. 2002 Apr; 51(4): 368-83. PMID 22449643.

3   Matson J.L., et al. DSM-VI vs DSM-5 diagnostic criteria for toddlers with autism. Dev Neurorehabil 2012; 15(3): 185-190. PMID 22582849.

tism Coordinating Committee in July 2012. The field trials for ASD were done at two pediatric sites and screened a total of 293 children ages 6-17. Of the 293 children screened by Dr. Swedo, 79 children qualified for an ASD diagnosis under the DSM-IV-TR criteria, and 64 qualified for an ASD diagnosis under the DSM-V criteria, which was a 19% decrease.

Despite the DSM-V's sleight-of-hand, autism is the fastest-growing serious developmental disability in the US, and it is clearly a major public health epidemic that is taking an enormous toll on millions of families across the country. In 2012, Autism Speaks, the world's leading autism science and advocacy organization, funded a study that estimated autism costs America a staggering $126 billion per year – a number that has more than tripled since 2006. The study, however, was based on the CDC's 2006 estimation for the prevalence of ASD – 1 in 110.

A 2012 study funded by Autism Speaks estimated the national cost of autism were around $137 annually. A 2014 Study Published in JAMA Pediatrics, concluded the average lifetime cost of supporting an individual with an ASD, and intellectual disability was $2.4 million.[4]

ASD has a greater prevalence than childhood cancer, juvenile diabetes, and pediatric AIDS combined. But the government funding on research for ASD pales in comparison to childhood cancer, juvenile diabetes, and pediatric AIDS. For example, in fiscal year 2014, the NIH estimates it will spend $190 million on autism research, but it will spend an estimated $192 million on pediatric AIDS research. The absurdity of the NIH expenditures regarding autism is illustrated when the children with HIV and the Americans with ASD are juxtaposed: An estimated 219 American children younger than 13 years of age in the US were diagnosed with HIV in 2010, and Autism Speaks estimates that over two million Americans are currently affected by autism!

In addition to the government giving short shrift to ASD, the American Psychiatric Association mutilated the

4   Buescher AV,: et al. Cost of autism spectrum disorders in the United Kingdom and the United States. JAMA Pediatrics 2014 Aug; 168(8): 721-8. PMID 24911948.

diagnosis of ASD via the DSM-V. Unfortunately, lurking just below the surface of the DSM-V is Big Pharma. A 2012 article in the PLoS Medical Journal exposed the financial ties between DSM-5 panel members and the pharmaceutical industry.[5] The article showed that nearly 70 percent of the DSM-V task-force members reported having ties to the pharmaceutical industry. This represents a relative increase of 20 percent over the proportion of *DSM-IV* task-force members with such ties just a decade ago. But it is not only task-force members who have financial relationships with Big Pharma. Of the 137 *DSM-V* panel members (or work-group members) who have posted disclosure statements, 77 (56 percent) reported industry ties, such as holding stock in pharmaceutical companies, serving as consultants to industry, or serving on company boards. Caught between the crossfire of the government and the interests of Big Pharma, autistic kids just can't seem to catch a break.

In addition to the nefarious influence of Big Pharma on the DSM-V, I would be remiss if I didn't mention that liar, thief, embezzler, and fugitive from justice Dr. Poul Thorsen was a member of the Neurodevelopmental Disorders Workgroup for the DSM-V, and he played an integral role in shaping the new and improved DSM-V ASD diagnosis.

---

5   Cosgrove L, Krimsy S. A comparison of DSM-IV and DSM-5 panel members financial associations with industry: a pernicious problem persists. PLoS Med 2012 March; 9(3): e1001190. PMCID: PMC 3302834.

Chapter Thirteen

Aborted Fetal Cell Vaccines

I believe that dad's crowning achievement was connecting with Theresa A. Deisher, Ph.D. I had the distinct pleasure of meeting her in 2012, when we participated in a 45 minute presentation, which was similar to the presentations she had given to congress, and the 2013 AutismOne conference in Chicago. Dr. Deisher obtained her Ph.D. in molecular and cellular physiology from Stanford University. She is the inventor of 23 U.S. patents, and the first person in the world to identify and patent stem cells from the human heart. She has spent over 19 years in commercial biotechnology, working with such pharma concerns as Genentech, Repligen, Zymo Genetics, Immunex, and Amgen. Although Dr. Deisher has rarified brilliance, she is a lovely, personable woman.

Dr. Deisher is the president and founder of Sound Choice Pharmaceutical Institute, a non-profit research and educational organization, dedicated to increasing awareness about the widespread and pervasive use of aborted fetal material in biomedical research and drug production. She is also the president of AVM Biotechnology, which seeks to patent and promote the use of fetal-free vaccines. Moreover, she was one of the keynote speakers at the 2013 Autism One-Generation Rescue Conference in Chicago.

Before the Minnesota Legislature on May 11th, 2012, Dr. Deisher said, "Over four years ago, it was obvious to my eye that autism disorder rates changed dramatically in certain specific years. Looking at autism disorder prevalence data from the United States Department of Education, it was clear that there were three specific years in which autism prevalence rose dramatically."

Dr. Deisher and the Sound Choice Pharmaceutical Institute performed a statistical analysis that demonstrated 1981, 1988, and 1996 were "changepoint" years for autism disorder. Changepoint years are not a year when the diagnosis of autism suddenly increased, but rather it is the year when children subsequently diagnosed with autism were born.

The CDC has acknowledged that a changepoint year for autism occurred in 1988. The CDC's acknowledgement was predicated on a study, "Timing of Increased Autistic Disorder Cumulative Incidents," published by EPA researchers in 2010.[1] Both the Sound Choice Pharmaceutical Institute and EPA studies used extremely stringent criteria for autism that only incorporated autism disorder as the sole criterion for the disorder. Their studies didn't include *pervasive developmental disorder*, Asperger syndrome, childhood disintegrative disorders, and Rett's syndrome, which were additional disorders that constituted ASD before the DSM-V.

Both the EPA and Sound Choice Pharmaceutical Institute studies also used California as a proxy for the autism rate in the U.S., but Sound Choice Pharmaceutical Institute used data gleaned from the Department of Education, whereas the EPA used data gleaned from the Department of Health and Human Services.

Although the EPA and Sound Choice Pharmaceutical Institute disagree on 1981 and 1996 as changepoint years, they concur that "changepoints" tell us that an environmental factor was introduced that triggered a sudden and dramatic rise in autism. The EPA is remiss in its identification of an environmental trigger, but Dr. Deisher has shown that the only universal factor associated with all three changepoints is the introduction of vaccines containing aborted fetal embryo cells.

1   Macdonald ME, Paul JF. Timing of increased autistic disorder cumulative incidence. Environ Sci Technol. 2010 Mar 15; 44(6): 2118-8. PMID 20158232.

According to Dr. Deisher, autism is a polygenetic disease, which means that a number of genes play a role in the development of autism – 300 different genes have been associated with autism. Having a mutation in one or more of the genes associated with autism does not invariably translate into a person developing the disorder. A polygenetic disease often requires an additional environmental trigger or triggers, and aborted fetal cell lines can serve as that trigger. Dr. Deisher's explanation accounts for the escalating autism rates in the U.S. even after the removal of most mercury-containing vaccines from the recommended vaccination schedule for children.

Dr. Deisher has illustrated the dangers of aborted fetal cell lines in vaccines and their potential for "insertional mutagenesis." Insertional mutagenesis is a term for the mutations that occur when foreign DNA is inserted into an organism's pre-existing DNA, as is the case with vaccines made from aborted fetal cell lines. Many of the vaccines administered to children contain retroviruses that integrate their DNA into the genome of their host. Human Endogenous Retrovirus K (HERVK), is a virus that is related to the MMLV virus. HERVK is also present in the MMRII vaccine, in Meruax, and in the chicken pox vaccine.[2] After the retrovirus' DNA has integrated into the cells of the host's DNA, it then starts to replicate, which can have an altering affect on the host's DNA.

Insertional mutagenesis has been observed in gene therapy, which uses retroviruses to deliver therapeutic DNA into a patient's cells. The most common form of gene therapy involves using DNA that encodes a functional, therapeutic gene to replace a mutated gene. Gene therapy with retroviruses has had varying degrees of success and also unintended, catastrophic consequences. For example, the New England Journal of Medicine published two clinical trials in 2002, and 2010. Both studies involved children with severe immunodeficiency, who are also known as Bubble Boys, because they have to live in sterile environments. All the children were treated with therapeutic genes that had been

2   Victoria J.G., et al. Viral Neucleic acids in live-attenuated vaccines: detection of minority variants an adventitious virus. J Virol. 2010June; 84(12): 6033-6040. PMCID: PMC2876658.

inserted in retroviruses. In the first study, three children were successfully treated, however a serious adverse event occurred in the fourth. As a result of the insertional mutagenesis event, which is considered to be low in humans.[3] The researches agreed that French authorities should halt their clinical trial, pending a thorough reassessment of the risks and benefits of continuing their gene therapy.[4]

In the second study nine children underwent similar insertional gene therapy. However, leukemia developed in four patients, and one died. In this clinical trail, a retrovirus similar to the MMLV virus caused inappropriate gene insertion, that led to the children's subsequent cancer.[5]

Additionally, the DNA fragments in the vaccines that contain aborted fetal cells are large enough to promote DNA disruption. In a paper, "Spontaneous Integration of Human DNA Fragments into Host Genome," presented at the International Society for Autism Research by Dr. Deisher, she demonstrated that vaccines contaminated by foreign DNA fragments and a retrovirus cause systemic inflammation and immune activation, which makes the host cell much more susceptible to incorporating the foreign DNA.[6] Dr. Deisher found that foreign DNA replaced up to 1% of an organisms' entire genome within just 30 minutes after its introduction into the organism. The results of her study regarding foreign DNA invading the host cell's DNA are consistent with a paper that was published in the Journal of Virology in 2010, which found that vaccines containing viruses and large DNA fragments invade the host cell's DNA en masse.[7]

3   Stocking C., et al. Distinct classes of factor-independent mutants can be isolated after retroviral mutagenesis of a human myeloid stem cell. Growth Factors. 1993; 8(3): 197-209. PMID: 8391284.
4   Hacein-Bey-Abina S., et al. A serious adverse event after successful gene therapy for X-linked severe combined immunodeficiency. N Engl J Med. 2003 Jan 16; 348(3): 255-6. PMID: 12529469.
5   Hacein-Bey-Abina S., Efficacy of gene therapy of X-linked severe combined immunodeficiency. N Engl J Med. 2010 Jul 22; 363(4): 355-64. PMID: 20660403.
6   s3.amazonaws.com/soundchoice/soundchoice/wp-content/uploads/2012/08/DNA_Contaminates_in_Vaccines_Can_Integrate_Into_Childrens_Genes.pdf.
7   Victoria J.G., et al. Viral neucleic acids in live attenuated vaccines: detection of minority variants and an adventitious virus. J Virol. 2010 June; 84(12): 6033-6040. PMCID: PMC2876658.

In 1979, the CDC and FDA unleashed the first vaccine derived from aborted human fetal cell lines on the American Public – Merck's Measles, Mumps, and Rubella Virus Vaccine Live (MMR). Merck's MMR vaccine has over 2 micrograms of residual double stranded human fetal DNA in each vaccine, which is approximately twice the amount of the active ingredient of the vaccine.

The CDC, FDA, and NIH had secretly approved switching from animal cell lines used in manufacturing vaccines to aborted human cell lines from second and third trimester pregnancies, and it took the CDC nearly twenty years to acknowledge that vaccines were incorporating aborted human fetal cells. Moreover, and unbelievably, no safety testing was ever performed on these vaccines when they were initiated. And currently in the U.S., over 10 vaccines are manufactured using human fetal cell lines.

Merck's MMR vaccine was licensed for use in children beginning at 12 months of age. After the MMR vaccine was introduced to children in 1979, the first changepoint identified by Dr. Deisher in 1981 occurred. In 1988, measles outbreaks caused a massive MMR vaccine compliance campaign that escalated MMR vaccination rates from 49% to over 82% by 1991. The escalation of the MMR vaccination rates in 1988 corresponds with the 1988 changepoint that was delineated by both Dr. Deisher and the CDC.

In 1995, the U.S. licensed Merck's Varivax varicella (chickenpox) vaccine. Like the MMR vaccine, the Varivax vaccine also uses fetal cell lines and is given to children aged 12 to18 months of age. Merck's Varivax vaccine was administered to children en masse starting in 1995, and Dr. Deisher's calculations show that 1996 is when the third autism changepoint year occurred. Similar associations between autism disorder changepoints and human fetal DNA-containing vaccines are evident in Canada, Denmark, Japan, and several Southeast Asian countries.

Earlier I mentioned that approximately 300 genes have been linked to autism, but oftentimes these genes require an external trigger to actually induce autism. But according to Deisher's research, vaccines may be solely responsible for creating autism in our children. Approximately 10% of autistic children in the U.S. have de novo autism, which means that their genetic mutations are not associated with inherited DNA from their parents.

The Interagency Autism Coordinating Committee (IACC), a branch of the Department of Health and Human Services, has embraced a scientific paper published in Nature that found these de novo mutations may be the result of advanced paternal age.[8] The study concluded that men fathering children later in life may not have genetic mutations that impart autism, but, rather, fathering children later in life has the potential to contribute to their offspring's unstable DNA and ultimately produce genetic mutations that engender de novo autism.

Dr. Deisher, however, has co-authored a paper, "Impact of Environmental Factors on the Prevalence of Autistic Disorder After 1979," that disputes the IACC's possible explanation for the skyrocketing rates of autism today.[9] The paper demonstrates that fathers over the age of 40 had similar numbers of live births in 1963 (333,785) as they did in 2001 (342,030), but the reported autism prevalence was 0.7 cases per 10,000 in 1963 compared to 79 per 10,000 in 2001. So Dr. Deisher and her colleagues ultimately concluded that paternal age was not a major trigger for autistic disorder, because older fathers would have been fathering as many autistic children in 1963 as 2008.

Regardless of where people stand on the pro-choice and pro-life choice divide regarding fetal cell derived vaccines, these vaccines derived from second and third trimester fetuses are producing autism in our children. During the 1980s and 1990s, American neonates, infants, and children

---

8   Kong A., et al. Rate of de novo mutations and the importance of fathers age to disease risk. Nature. 2012 Aug 23; 488(7412): 471-5. PMID: 22914163 PM-CID: PMC3548427.

9   Deisher T.A., et al. Impact of environmental factors on the prevalence of autistic disorder after 1979. Journal of Public Health and Epidemiology. 2014 Sep; 6(9): 271-286.

www.academicjournals.org/journal/JPHE/article-abstract/C98151247042. Full text pdf.

were subjected to two ever enlarging and deleterious trends: vaccines containing fetal cell line and vaccines containing ethylmercury. When these two trends are superimposed on each other, the genesis of America's autistic holocaust becomes quite evident.

Chapter 14

GMOs and Autism

An additional trend that may be contributing to the autistic holocaust is the widespread consumption of genetically modified (GM) foods, because they have the potential to exacerbate the gastrointestinal disorders that affect autistic children and may also exacerbate autism by hindering digestive function and the ability to process nutrients. As I discussed in Chapter 10, Dr. John Walker-Smith found a relationship among the MMR vaccine, ASD, and gastrointestinal disorders in 1996.

And a number of studies have since corroborated that autistic children are prone to high rates of gastrointestinal disorders. For example, a 2006 article, published in the Journal of Developmental and Behavioral Pediatrics, concluded that children with ASD have a higher rate of gastrointestinal (GI) symptoms than children with typical development. GI symptoms were elicited in 70 percent of children with ASD, compared to 28 percent of children with typical development.[1] A 2011 study published in BioMed Central Gastroenterology, concluded that the strong correlation of GI symptoms with autism severity indicates that children with more severe autism are likely to have more severe GI symptoms and visa-versa. Furthermore, autism symptoms are probably exacerbated due to the underlying gastrointestinal problems.[2]

---

1   Valicenti-McDermmott M., et al. Frequency of gastrointestinal symptoms in children with autism spectrum disorders and association with family history of autoimmune disease. J Dev Behav Pediatr. 2006 Apr; 27(2 suppl): S128-36. PMID: 16685179.

2   Adams J.B., et al. Gastrointestinal flora and gastrointestinal states in chil-

GMOS AND AUTISM

As the rate of ASD was escalating in the 1990s, Americans intake of GM foods was also escalating. According to the United States Department of Agriculture, GM foods entered the U.S. market in 1994 and by 2012 more than 93 percent of all soy planted in the U.S. was genetically engineered, and 73 percent of all U.S. corn now is genetically modified. The sweetener aspartame (NutraSweet) and rennet used to make cheeses also contain genetically modified organisms (GMOs). So genetically modified foods and organisms are almost ubiquitous in the American diet.

Monsanto, the company that gave us the deadly Agent Orange, is the primary producer of GM seeds that reap GM crops, and many of the GM crops that spring from Monsanto's GM seeds are resilient to the Monsanto's Roundup herbicide, which contains glyphosate. Despite Monsanto propaganda that lauds Roundup to be safe and its benefits to be on par with the Second Coming, numerous studies have demonstrated that glyphosate is toxic to mammals and several countries have banned various GMOs.

The currently accepted dogma in the U.S. is that glyphosate is not harmful to humans or to any mammals because the bio-molecular mechanisms that it disrupts—the shikimate pathway—is absent in mammals. However, this pathway is present in the gut bacteria of humans, and it plays an important role in human physiology, because the bacteria it produces aids digestion and detoxification, synthesizes vitamins, participates in immune system function, and also gastrointestinal tract permeability. Additionally, glyphosphate is purged by glutathione, which is significantly depleted in many autistic individuals, so its toxicity is exacerbated among a significant cross-section of people afflicted by ASD. (In Chapter 9, I discussed glutathione deficiencies among individuals with ASD). Moreover, studies have shown that glyphosate is toxic to the liver, and it has been also speculated that glyphosate's impairment of liver function can be particularly toxic

dren with autism- comparisons to typical children and correlation with autism severity. BMC Gastroenterology. 2011; 11: 22. PMCID: PMC 3072352.

129

to people afflicted with autism, because it hinders their digestive function and ability to process nutrients.

Various GM seeds and consequently crops also contain Bacillus thuringiensis (or Bt), a bacteria that is designed to kill insects by producing holes in their digestive tracts. After the insects ingest Bt, its spores spill out of their gut and germinate in the insect, causing death within a couple days. Monsanto and the government claim that Bt toxins are innocuous to humans. But, a 2011 study published in Reproductive Toxicology demonstrated that Bt toxins have been found in pregnant women. This was the first study to reveal the presence of circulating pesticides associated to genetically modified food.[3] A second study, published in the Journal of Applied Toxicology, found that Bt toxins target human embryonic cells.[4] Although, it has yet to be determined whether or not Bt seeds and crops erode the integrity of humans' gastrointestinal tracts, leading to widespread gut permeability and dysfunction. Researchers published a study in Natural Toxins demonstrating that mice fed with GM potatoes suffered subsequent intestinal tissue damage. The researchers added a warning, that thorough testing of these types of genetically engineered crops must be made, to avoid the risks before marketing.[5]

In addition to affecting the digestive tract, GM foods have been implicated in adverse physiological reactions in rats. Irina Ermakova, PhD, a senior researcher at the Russian Academy of Sciences, reported to the European Congress of Psychiatry in 2006 that GM soy-fed female rats had a 50 percent higher mortality rate than pups from control groups that were not fed GM soy. A third of GM soy-fed female rat pups were sick and weighed much less than pups from the

3 Aris A., Leblanc S. Maternal and fetal exposure to pesticides associated to genetically modified foods in Eastern Townships of Quebec, Canada. Repro Toxicol. 2001 May; 31(4); 528-33. PMID: 21338670.

4 Mesnage R., et al. Cytotoxicity on human cells of Cry1Ab and Cry1Ac Bt insecticidal toxins alone or with a glyphosate-based hebicide. Journal Applied Toxicology. 2012 Feb 15. onlinelibrary.wiley.com/doi/10.1002/jat.2712/abstract.

5 Fares N.H., El-Sayed A.K. Fine structural changes in the ileum of mice fed on delta-endotoxin-treated potatoes and transgenic potatoes. Nat Toxins. 1998; 6(6): 219-233. PMID: 10441029.

control groups. Her data also showed a high level of anxiety and aggression in rats from the GM-soy group: GM-soy fed females and rat pups attacked and bit each other. The latter antisocial and aggressive behaviors are consistent with the behaviors of a cross-section of autistic children.

Unfortunately, speaking out about the deleterious effects of GM foods can be equally hazardous to a career as speaking out about the deleterious effects of vaccines, and world renowned biochemist and nutritionist Arpad Pusztai, Ph.D., is a case in point. In 1998, Dr. Pusztai declared that the king was naked when he publicly announced that his research on rats fed GM potatoes suffered negative effects to their stomach linings and immune system. After Dr. Pusztai publicly announced his findings, he was expunged from the prestigious Rowett Research Institute in the UK and publicly excoriated by the Royal Society of Medicine. His career then followed the same downward trajectory as the careers of Drs. Wakefield and Geier.

In fact, Big Agro and Big Pharma share a number of ruthless and predatory traits when it comes to silencing their critics and also with regards to their cozy relationships to government entities that should oversee and regulate them. Big Agro includes the multi-national corporations Monsanto, Cargil, and ConAgra, but Monsanto unequivocally epitomizes the sheer malevolence of Big Agro.

Amazingly, a former managing director of Monsanto's India operations, Tiruvadi Jagadisan, blew the whistle on the government of India's acquiescence to Monsanto regarding the company's GM Bt eggplant seeds. He stated publicly that Monsanto submitted "fake scientific data" to the Indian government regulatory agencies to receive commercial approvals for its products in India. Jagadisan also said that the Indian government simply accepted the data provided by Monsanto without questioning its veracity.

Jagadisan felt compelled to speak out about the utter carnage that Monsanto had inflicted throughout India. In the 1980s, India had very strict regulations regarding GM seeds, but the World Bank pressured the Indian government to deregulate its seed market with catastrophic results. The exorbitant cost of Monsanto's seeds and the other chemicals the seeds required pushed many Indian farmers into an extreme debt trap, which precipitated the suicide of over 200,000 Indian farmers. In 2012, the Indian Supreme Court recommended a 10-year moratorium on field trials of all GM food and termination of all ongoing trials of transgenic crops, but by 2012 the devastation wrought by Monsanto was irrevocable.

Although the Indian government wised up to the destructive effects of GM crops, and several nations have banned various GM crops, the U.S. FDA hasn't been inclined to protect Americans from GMOs. The FDA doesn't even require GM foods marketed in the U.S. to be labeled, even though every country in the European Union and also Japan, Russia and China require GM foods to be labeled. Several polls, including an ABC News poll, have demonstrated that more than 90 percent of Americans believe that GM foods should at least be labeled, but the FDA hasn't been inclined to act on those beliefs.

Because the FDA refuses to budge about labeling GM foods, the individual states have been forced to address this matter. Vermont has passed a GMO labeling law that will take effect in 2016. Connecticut and Maine have also passed GMO labeling laws, but their legislation contains provisions stating that the laws can't be implemented until several other states approve similar labeling laws. Moreover, legislation requiring GM foods to be labeled is currently wending through the legislatures of several states.

Unfortunately, when the citizens of states have voted on whether or not they require GM foods to be labeled, they're confronted by an extremely well financed propaganda juggernaut that is mounted by Monsanto et al. According to the Washington, D.C.-based Center for Food Safety, chemical, agricultural and large food companies have spent over $100 million in four US states—Oregon, Colorado, California and Washington—to ensure that the citizens of those states do not enact GMO labeling laws.

The vote in Washington state was extremely close—51 percent to 49 percent—in favor of no GMO labeling. The proponents of labeling raised about $8.4 million, and the proponents of no labeling poured more than $22 million into their campaign. The proponents of labeling GMO foods raised $2.6 million within the state of Washington, and the proponents of no labeling only managed to raise $550 within the state. To avoid consumer outrage, the Grocery Manufacturers Association of America, "a trade association of the food industry," laundered the donations of the multinational corporations that flooded the coffers of the no labeling proponents.

Big Agro, like Big Pharma, has the funding and clout to subvert the political process. The clout of Monsanto was exemplified by the Consolidated and Further Continuing Appropriations Act of 2013. The Act that was passed by the U.S. Congress to prevent the shutdown of the federal government by authorizing the funding for a multitude of federal agencies, but it also contained the "Farmer Assurance Provision," which was a "rider" or an additional provision that has little or no connection to the actual subject matter of a bill. (Politicians often sneak pork barrel spending or malfeasant legislation into riders of much larger bills or legislation.)

The Farmer Assurance Provision has been called the "Monsanto Protection Act," because it barred U.S. federal courts from being able to prevent the sale or planting of GMO crops even if they failed to meet federal safety standards or were discovered to be harmful to humans or the environment. In other words, Monsanto, and other Big Agro conglomerates, are able to continue selling seeds that have not yet faced adequate testing to assess their health and environmental impacts by eliminating the ability for a substantive challenge in federal court. In chapter 6, I discussed how the National Vaccine Injury Compensation Program protects Big Pharma from being sued by the parents of vaccine-injured children in federal court, and the Farmer Assurance Provision is similar in the sense that it protects Big Agro in our federal courts.

In Chapter 6, I also discussed the revolving door between the government and Big Pharma and how a myriad of government officials who have pledged to serve and protect American citizens from the taint and corruption of Big Pharma have abrogated their responsibilities and seamlessly segued into prestigious and lucrative careers with Big Pharma. Big Agro has access to the same revolving door and that revolving door has been instrumental in ensuring that GM foods have never been tested for safety. Yes, indeed, believe it or not, GM foods have never been tested for safety!

Michael Taylor has spent nearly three decades in the revolving door between government and Big Agro, and he has played an integral role in exempting GM foods from FDA scrutiny. Taylor served as an FDA staff lawyer and Executive Assistant to the FDA Commissioner from 1976 to 1981, and then, lo and behold, in 1981, he skipped into the private sector when he joined law firm that represented Monsanto. After ten years of representing Monsanto, he passed though the revolving yet again and was incarnated as the Deputy Commissioner for Policy at the FDA.

During Taylor's second stint at the FDA, he oversaw the FDA's policy on GM foods, which consisted of the FDA declaring that GM foods didn't require safety testing, because they are "generally recognized as safe" or GRAS. The FDA justified this claim on the assumption that GM crops contain "the same as or substantially similar" to substances found in non-GM foods. The GRAS policy was initially implemented in the 1950s—decades before the advent of GM foods.

Thus, Michael Taylor had directly segued from working for Monsanto to the FDA and implementing a radical new regulatory framework that clearly benefited his former client. Luckily, a few members of Congress were privy to Taylor's glaring conflict of interest, and they called for the Government Accountability Office to conduct an ethics investigation into Taylor's actions at the FDA. The investigation concluded that Taylor had violated ethics rules 11 times, but that "there were no conflicting financial interests." That assumption, however, proved to be premature, because Taylor left the government in 1998 and was appointed Monsanto's vice president for public policy. In 2009, Taylor passed through the revolving door yet again, when President Obama appointed him to be Deputy Commissioner for Foods for the FDA.

I would be remiss if I didn't mention Michael A. Friedman, who served as Deputy Commissioner of Policy and also acting Commissioner of the FDA under the Clinton presidency, and, when he left the FDA, he was then anointed Senior Vice President of Clinical Affairs at Phamacia, a pharmaceutical conglomerate that included Upjohn and Searle, which at the time, was owned by Monsanto. Monsanto has since sold the Pharmacia Corporation to Pfizer, the largest pharmaceutical company in the world. Unfortunately, Taylor and Friedman are just two examples among many of the nepotism that exists between the government and Big Agro.

Earlier in the chapter, I discussed how Monsanto's Roundup has glyphosate, which severely affects bacteria in the gut, causing impaired immune system function. Several researchers have demonstrated that individuals with autism are in a state of perpetual viral or bacterial infection. For example, a 2005 paper published in the Annals of Neurology examined autopsied brain tissues of 11 individuals with autism and also the cerebrospinal fluid of six living autistic patients and found that individuals with autism had a marked increase in inflammatory reactions in the brain that are indicative of chronic infection.[6] A 1998 study published in Clinical Immunology and Immunopathology has also shown an association between high levels of virus serology in autism, and the study's authors felt that their results supported the hypothesis that a virus-induced autoimmune response may play a causative role in autism.[7] Moreover,

6   Vargas D.L., et al Neurological activation and neuroinflammation in the brain of patients with autism. Ann Neurol. 2005 Jan; 57(1): 67-81. PMID: 15546155.
7   Singh V.K., Lin S.X., Yang V.C. Serological association of measles virus and human herpesvirus-6 with brain autoantibodies in autism. Clin Immunol Im-

a 2002 paper published in a prestigious medical journal, Clinical Infectious Diseases, found that children with autism are significantly more susceptible to Clostridia, a species of bacteria, than children without autism.[8]

Science linking chronic viral and bacterial infection to autism is a silver lining to very dark cloud. I believe it's a silver lining, because treating autistic children for chronic infection has yielded astonishing results in many cases. Stan Kurtz is not a doctor or a scientist, but, rather, he's the father of an autistic son, and he was able to reverse his son's autism by a diet and protocol that was designed to treat underlying viral and bacterial infections.

The diet and protocol developed by Kurtz eliminates all GMO products in favor of organic products, and it also eliminates gluten and casein—the latter are proteins found in mammalian milk. Gluten and casein have been shown to leak from the gut and cause autoimmune issues. In addition, Kurtz gave his son the antiviral Valtrex, the antifungal Diflucan, and probiotics. Valtrex and Diflucan treated underlying infections and the probiotics corrected an imbalance of natural bacteria in the digestive tract. Moreover, Kurtz incorporated a myriad of vitamins and nutritional supplements into the protocol that cured his son of autism. If readers are interested in Kurtz's revolutionary approach, they should browse his website: stankurtz.com.

munopathol. 1998 Oct; 89(1): 105-8. PMID: 9756729.

8   Finegold S.M., et al. Gastrointestinal microflora studies in late-onset autism. Clin Infect Dis. 2002 Sep1; 35(Suppl 1): S6-S16. PMID: 12173102.

CHAPTER 15

CLOSING THOUGHTS

W riting *The Autistic Holocaust* has been a heart-breaking odyssey. In many respects, the odyssey started when my son was born—more than 28 years ago. And the impetus for writing the book was the knowledge I acquired while working for my father, which was certainly a crash course on autism, government corruption, and Big Pharma's willful negligence in light of a national crisis.

Throughout this odyssey, I've met a number of truly amazing people who include scientists, autism advocates, and, of course, the parents or siblings of children who have been the victims of a vaccine injury. The sheer numbers of people who have been affected by autism have often overwhelmed me.

Early on in the book, I discussed the first grand myth the government has manufactured about vaccines: Jonas Salk's eradication of polio. I also mentioned that the Salk and Sabin vaccines were laced with simian virus 40, a human carcinogen that was administered to millions of children, and how the CDC has covered up the role of simian virus 40 as a contributing factor in cancer. So the government lying to Americans about vaccines isn't a new fangled fad.

I also discussed several scientific studies that have linked thimerosal-containing ethylmercury to autism, even though the U.S. government has categorically denied the link. Moreover, researchers who have exposed the link—like Drs. Andrew Wakefield and Mark Geier—have been publicly crucified, which has sent a very resounding message to the medical community to snap into line concerning vaccines.

Although thimerosal is indisputably toxic and certainly one of the causes of the autism pandemic, Dr. Theresa Deisher, who I discussed in Chapter 13, points out that the vast majority of vaccines with thimerosal were phased out in 2002, but the autism pandemic continues to proliferate. I think that her data on "change-point years," where the blight of autism rose dramatically when various vaccines containing aborted fetal cell lines were introduced into our children's vaccine schedule is quite compelling. My hope is that additional scientists look into Dr. Deisher's credible research, because our children are currently being inundated by vaccines that contain aborted fetal cell lines.

Although this book has many disturbing aspects, I think probably the most disturbing facet is the synergistic corruption between the government and Big Pharma that enables the autistic holocaust to flourish unabated. Throughout the course of this book, I've shown multiple instances where the government has lied to protect the interests of Big Pharma.

I think one of the most egregious examples of a government official lying to protect the interests of Big Pharma regarding vaccines was when the CDC's Dr. Colleen Boyle perjured herself before the Committee on Oversight and Government Reform. After Dr. Boyle played an integral role in helping to misrepresent the data contained in the Verstraeten study, she said the following before the Committee: "The CDC is actively involved in detecting and investigating vaccine safety concerns and supporting a wide range of vaccine safety research to address safety questions."

The emails among Verstraeten and his CDC superiors to misrepresent the CDC's vaccine data have since become public record, because of the Freedom of Information Act, so Dr. Boyles' lies have been unabashedly exposed. But, yet, Dr. Boyle hasn't been charged with perjury. In fact, the CDC rewarded her perjury before Congress by promoting her to the CDC's Associate Director for Science and Public Health at the National Center on Birth Defects and Developmental Disabilities.

Unfortunately, the Prescription Drug User Fee Act (PDUFA), enacted in 1992 under the George H.W. Bush administration, primed Americans for a disturbing relationship between their government and Big Pharma. As I mentioned in Chapter 6, PDUFA enables Big Pharma to pay fees directly to the FDA, so it can sidestep standard FDA rules and regulations when ushering new drugs to market.

In Chapter 6, I also showed just how perfidious the relationship between the government and Big Pharma had become when I commented on the plight of David Graham, MD, MPH, the Associate Director for Science and Medicine at the FDA's Office of Drug Safety, who spoke out about a drug, Vioxx, that killed thousand of Americans because of the falsified data of Big Pharma conglomerate Merck. Before a Senate subcommittee, Dr. Graham testified that when his team concluded its study on Vioxx and prepared to present its results, it was attacked by various sectors of the FDA, and he feared the loss of his job. Dr. Graham's travails demonstrate that government scientists and officials are now afraid to speak out against Big Pharma.

The revolving door between government and Big Pharma, and Big Agro for that matter, is also extremely disturbing, because it allows government officials to make decisions that are deleterious to the American public, and be greatly rewarded by multinational corporate interests when they leave the government. For example, as CDC Director, Julie Gerberding had been a champion of vaccines, and when she left the CDC, she became the president of Merck, a major producer of vaccines. Moreover, former NIH Director Elias Zerhouni left his government position and now heads Big Pharma bellwether Sanofi, a major producer of vaccines.

The National Childhood Vaccine Injury Act, which banned the parents of vaccine-injured children from suing vaccine manufacturers, is a breathtaking travesty of justice, and it epitomizes the corrupt partnership between the government and Big Pharma. The National Vaccine Injury Compensation Program (VICP) was created under the National Childhood Vaccine Injury Act to institute a no-fault, non-adversarial alternative to suing vaccine manufacturers, and it has mass-produced injustice after injustice. The Homeland

Security Act also allows pharmaceutical companies to escape liability lawsuits by invoking the red herring that such litigation infringes on national security. The autistic holocaust that America is currently enduring will only become horrifically worse until the unethical and crooked relationship between the government and Big Pharma is severed.

U.S. Representative Dan Burton witnessed the deleterious effects of vaccines firsthand: His grandson was a normal, healthy infant until he received nine vaccinations in one day during his second year of life. Two days after his grandson received the series of vaccinations, he became withdrawn, started to cry endlessly, and bang his head against the wall. Since then, his grandson has been diagnosed with autism.

Representative Burton was fully cognizant of the deleterious effects of vaccines, and he was also one of the most powerful congressmen in Washington, because he chaired the House's Committee on Oversight and Government Reform. Between April of 2000 and May of 2004 Representative Burton initiated nine hearings on autism and vaccines before the Committee on Oversight and Government Reform, which ultimately produced a number of scathing reports linking mercury to autism. Despite Congressman Burton's heroic efforts, he was unable to dent the monolith of lies and deception that has been constructed by the CDC, FDA, NIH, and Big Pharma. He retired from the House in disgust after a stellar 30-year career in Congress.

In Chapter 12 of the book, I dispelled the popular lie that the explosive growth of autism is due to an ever increasing definition of its symptoms. In reality, the symptoms that define autism according to the Diagnostic and Statistical Manual: Mental Disorders (DSM) were scaled back in 2000, and the DSM-V, published in 2013 eviscerated the symptoms that entail ASD. The DSM-V removed Asperger syndrome and pervasive developmental disorder-not otherwise specified from its classification for ASD. The DSM-V now requires more total symptoms to be met in the areas of social/communication deficits and repetitive/

restrictive behaviors than the DSM-IV-TR, which started to restrict the symptoms of ASD in 2000. In Chapter 12, I also discussed how Big Pharma is in a position to skew DSM task force members' beliefs, because the majority of them report having financial ties to Big Pharma.

But despite the modifications to the DSM that limits the number of children being diagnosed with ASD, their numbers continue to swell. As of 2014, 1 in 68 American children were diagnosed with ASD—compared to 1 in 150 in 2002. For Americans to overcome the current autistic holocaust, their government will have to become honest and discontinue covering up the devastation wrought by Big Pharma.

Writing *The Autistic Holocaust* has been a dark odyssey into government and corporate corruption and untold suffering, but over the course of it I've reunited with my son, Jon, which has been the wellspring of indescribable joy. I've learned a great deal about my son since our reunion on December 11th, 2013. Jon is loving, thoughtful, and he has tremendous insight. He understands that his ASD does not define his character, but he also recognizes his limitations and operates within them on a daily basis.

Although it's important to discover a cure for autism, I feel that it's equally important to accept every child for who they are. Some families, and some children, will certainly face far greater challenges than others, but loving Jon for who he is has been tremendously liberating for me.

Today I see a talented young man instead of a child with a disability. The animosity I've harbored towards the government and Big Pharma for poisoning our children has taken a backseat to the acceptance I've nurtured for my son. There is no disability that could ever diminish my acceptance of him. The injustices seem ubiquitous and the fight for justice seems never ending, but now Jon and I can face the challenges together.

April is National Autism Awareness month. This year I'll be participating in my third annual "Walk for Autism Awareness," hosted by the E. John Gavras Center in Auburn,

N.Y.. The Center's inaugural walk for autism in 2013 was a tremendous success, which ballooned in size the following year. Naturally, a gauntlet of red corrugated signs with white lettering are posted all along the way. They present some cold hard facts about autism. The harsh weather of an early spring simply reinforces those cold hard corrugated facts. Then again, having endured one of the coldest, and snowiest winters in recorded history, I gladly welcome a spring snow shower. For one day in April we can all stand, walk, and face the challenges of autism together as a community.

NATIONAL ORGANIZATIONS FOR AUTISM TREATMENT AND ADVOCACY

Autism Research Institute (ARI)
4182 Adams Ave.
San Diego California 92116
Toll Free: 866-366-3361
Steven Edelson Ph.D. Executive Director
www.autismresearchinstitute.com

The Autism Research Institute (ARI) is a non-profit organization focused on conducting and sponsoring research aimed at improving the quality of life for today's generation of children and adults with ASD. ARI was established in 1967 by Dr. Bernard Rimland, who single-handedly destroyed the claim that autism was caused by poor parenting in his 1964 book Infantile Autism. Between 1960 and 1980 ARI focused much of its efforts on disseminating information on behavioral therapy and nutritional and dietary interventions for ASD. Since Dr. Rimland's death, ARI continues to follow his vision, as well as cultivating new ground-breaking initiatives for individuals with ASD. Dr. Bernard Rimland also founded the Autism Society of America.

Medical Academy of Pediatric Special Needs (MAPS)

16251 Laguana Canyon Rd #175
Irvine, California 92618
Toll Free: 855-447-4200
Fax: 307-213-1401
inquiry@medmaps.org

The Medical Academy of Pediatric Special Needs (MAPS) mission is to prepare medical professionals to deliver the best possible care to children with ASD and other special needs. The organization is comprised of a group physicians and scientists who have joined together with the mission of evaluating and disseminating practical research and evidence-based treatments for ASD. The MAPS Fellowship Program at the Medical Academy of Pediatric Special Needs is an accredited Continuing Medical Education program that is designed to prepare medical professionals to deliver the best possible care to children in distress. MAPS is also working with leading pediatric research institutes and recruiting medical and scientific experts in the fields of ASD and environmental medicine to further develop its in-depth CME approved curriculum.

The Autism Society

4340 East-West Hwy
Suite 35
Bethesda, Maryland 20814
Toll Free: 800-328-8476
info@autism-sociey.org
President/Chief Executive Officer- Scott Badesh

The Autism Society staff is made up of individuals with ASD, parents, siblings, and their supporters, and it was founded in 1965 by Bernard Rimland, Ph.D. In 1968, Ruth Sullivan became the organization's first elected president. The Society has grown from a handful of parents into a leading source of information, research, reference, and support and is the largest grassroots organization within the autism community. The Autism Society convened its first national conference on autism in 1969, and its advocacy efforts have played a key role in the passage of the Individuals with Disabilities Education Act. The Society's board of directors is comprised of volunteer representatives, many of whom are parents of autistic children. Individuals with ASD have also served on the organization's Board, and played key rolls in the organization. Today the Society has more than 120,000 members and supporters who are connected through a network of more than 115 nationwide affiliates.

National Vaccine Information Center (NVIC)
21525 Ridgetop Circle, Suite 100
Sterling, Virginia 20166
Phone: 703-938-0342
Fax: 571-313-1268
President/ Barbara Loe Fisher
www.nvic.org

The National Vaccine Information Center (NVIC) is a charitable, non-profit educational organization founded in 1982. The NVIC launched the vaccine safety and informed consent movement in America in the 1980's, and it is the oldest and largest consumer led organization advocating for the institution of vaccine safety and informed consent protections in the public health system. The organization provides assistance to those who have suffered vaccine injuries, and it promotes and funds research to evaluate vaccine safety and effectiveness. The NVIC also monitors vaccine research, development, regulation, policy-making, and legislation. Since 1982, the NVIC has advocated that scientific studies on vaccines are conducted that define the various biological mechanisms involved in their instigation of injury and death. The organization has also advocated that studies identify genetic and other biological high risk factors for those who suffer chronic brain and immune system dysfunction following a vaccination.

Vaccine Liberation Army (VLA)
Director & Co-Founder: Eileen Dannemann
Fairfield, Iowa
Phone: 319-855-0307
ncowmail@gmail.com

The VLA is committed to disseminating information about the risks and dangers of vaccines. For many years the VLA's focus has been on non-industry, non-government driven research on the safety and effectiveness of vaccinations. The VLA's Director and Co-founder Eileen Dannemann points out that there are over 5,000 studies that substantiate and verify the dangers and risks of vaccines and their components, such as mercury, aluminum, and aborted fetal cell lines. The VLA also opposes the public media campaigns that support the benefits of vaccines but ignore their risks.

AutismOne
1816 West Houston Drive
Fullerton, California 92853
Toll Free: 800-908-5803
fax: 714-441-9327
Ed Arranga Co-Founder & President
Terri Arranga Executive Director
info@autismone.org

Ed Arranga and Terri Arranga are married and the founders of AutismOne. The driving force behind their organization is the fact that they have a child with autism. AutismOne and its initiatives educate more than 100,000 families every year about autism prevention, recovery, safety, and change. AutismOne Radio is a world-wide based radio station with shows hosted by Terri Arranga, addressing all the pressing issues of autism. Every year in Chicago, AutismOne hosts the largest and most comprehensive conference on autism in the world.

UNLOCKING AUTISM
P.O. Box 208
Tyrone, Georgia 30290
Toll Free: 866-366-3361
President/Shelly Hendrix
Vice President/Nancy Cole
unlockingautism.org

Shortly after Shelly Hendrix's two-year-old son Liam was diagnosed with autism in 1998, she and her husband co-founded Unlocking Autism. Unlocking Autism has grown out of a concern that children were being diagnosed with ASD at an alarming rate, and yet the public was uninformed about their plight. Their primary mission is to bring the issues of autism from individual homes to the forefront of national dialogue. Unlocking Autism consistently strives to bring parents and professionals together in one concerted effort to fight for children with ASD. Its mission includes educating parents about the available biomedical treatments, pending legislation, and existing laws, as well as raising funds for biomedical and behavioral research projects to help those on the autism spectrum reach their greatest potential.

Moms Against Mercury
55 Carson's Trail
Leicester, North Carolina 28748
Phone: 828-776-0082
www.momsagainstmercury.com
President & Founder/Amy M. Carson

Moms Against Mercury (MAM) is a nonprofit organization dedicated to raising awareness and educating the public on the dangerous use of thimerosal. MAM's founder Amy M. Carson has been an advocate for safer vaccines for several years, after her son became injured by them. She has organized and moderated numerous national and state assemblies and press conferences to bring attention to the urgent need to remove all forms of mercury from pharmaceuticals. She has worked side by side with members of Congress and world-renowned researchers and scientists. MAM board member Boyd E. Haley, PhD., received a doctorate in Chemistry/Biochemistry at Washington State University, and he has testified before numerous government agencies on the effects of mercury toxicity from dental amalgums and vaccines. Dr. Haley was one of the first researchers to propose that the preservative thimerosal in infant vaccines was the most likely toxic agent involved in the Gulf War Syndrome and autism related disorders.

SafeMinds
(Sensible Alternatives For Elimination of Mercury in Drugs)
P.O. Box 285
Huntington Beach, California 92648
404-934-0777
Co-founder & President/ Sallie Bernard
Vice President & Co Chair/Lyn Redwood
www.safeminds.org

SafeMinds' platform is that the epidemic of childhood autism and the disabilities that accompany autism will end when our environment, food, and health care products are universally safe and non-toxic. The organization has established a link between mercury and autism through the landmark paper, "Autism, A Novel Form of Mercury Poisoning." SafeMinds is also the driving force behind scientific research that links environmental factors, such as mercury, to autism. The organization has sponsored nearly $1.5 million in research related specifically to mercury and adverse neurological outcomes, making it the largest private non-profit organization for funding mercury and autism-related research. SafeMinds also works for justice, accountability and integrity in science and public policy. Sallie Bernard, SafeMinds' co-founder and president, has testified before Congress, presented to the Institute of Medicine, published a number of research papers and letters in science journals, and participates in several government committees addressing the effect of mercury on neurodevelopment.

Talk About Curing Autism (TACA)
National Office: 2222 Martin St., Suite 140
Irvine, California 92612
Toll Free: 855-726-7810
Fax: 949-640-4424
President/Glen Ackerman
Founder & Secretary/Lisa Ackerman
www.tacanow.org

Talk About Curing Autism (TACA) is a national, non-profit organization dedicated to educating, empowering and supporting families affected by autism. For families whose children have recently received an ASD diagnosis, TACA endeavors to speed up the process between the autism diagnosis and effective treatments. The organization also helps to strengthen the autism community by connecting families and professionals. In 2013, TACA maintained a chapter presence in 21 states, and its monthly meetings include expert speakers on a variety of autism related topics. The organization also offers parents additional educational opportunities, including its Autism Journey Seminars, Special Education Law Lectures & Clinics, and REAL HELP NOW Conferences, which focus on autism related topics like advocacy, medical issues, and feature special expert guest speakers from around the United States.

National Autism Association (NAA)
One Park Avenue, Suite 1
Porstmouth, Rhode Island 02871
Toll Free: 877-622-2884
Local: 401-293-5551
Fax: 401-293-5342
Co-Founder, Executive Director/ Lori McIlwain
President, Founding Board Member/Wendy Fournier
naa@nationalautism.org

The National Autism Association (NAA) is a nonprofit, parent-run advocacy organization, and its mission is to respond to the most urgent needs of the autism community by providing tangible help and hope. The NAA has become a leading voice on urgent issues related to severe autism, regressive autism, autism safety, autism abuse, and crisis prevention. The organization has adopted the position that genetic predispositions and susceptibilities play a role in the development of autism, but environmental interactions play a much larger role. So the NAA supports cutting-edge research that studies environmental triggers responsible for creating the tipping point in genetically susceptible children, as well as promising treatment options. In response to the growing needs of families and professionals impacted by autism, the NAA assembled a National Autism Conference in St. Pete Beach, Florida, November of 2014, which included some of the world's most renowned experts in cutting edge research on environmental toxins, dietary intervention, and legal and legislative strategies.

Autism Action Network (AAN)
550 East Chester Street
Long Beach, N.Y. 11561
Phone: 516-382-0081
Fax (888) 995-6161
Executive Director/John Gilmore
jgilmore@autismactionnetwork.org

The Autism Action Network (AAN) is a national, non-partisan political action organization whose mission is to be a strong and unified voice for people with neurodevelopmental and communication disorders. The parents of children who suffered from vaccine injuries, neurodevelopmental disorders, and communication disorders formed the AAN, and it's dedicated to advancing public policy issues affecting people with autism and related disorders. The AAN supports candidates who share their goals in state and federal elections, because one of its objectives is to hold the government accountable. The organization is continually striving to advance policies that are germane to ASD, including education, health insurance coverage, and legal and legislative issues.

Generation Rescue
13636 Ventura Blvd., Suite 259
Sherman Oaks, California 91423
President/Jenny McCarthy
Executive Director/ Candace McDonald
Toll Free: 877-98 AUTISM
877-982-8847
Fax: 818-990-0044
www.generationrescue.org

Generation Rescue is a leading national organization that provides hope, information, and immediate treatment assistance for families affected by ASD. The organization supports families affected by autism in numerous ways, including programs on autism treatment, a free national conference, and also virtual and local conferences. Generation Rescue also offers parent mentors, which are affectionately referred to as "Rescue Angels." Rescue Angels are a network of over 1,300 parents of children diagnosed with autism in 38 countries, who have seen significant improvement in their children and volunteer their time to answer questions, give guidance, and provide referrals to families in need. The organization also provides a list of recommended physicians, medical grants for families who cannot afford critical treatments, and nutritional counseling. Hollywood actress and New York Times best-selling author Jenny McCarthy is currently the president of Generation Rescue—she is also the mother of a son with autism.

Coalition for Mercury-Free Drugs, Inc. CoMeD
14 Redgate Court
Silver Spring, Maryland 20905-5726
General inquiries: Info@Mercury-FreeDrugs.org.

President/Lisa K. Sykes: Lisa@Mercury-freeDrugs.org
Vice President/David A. Geier: David@Mercury-freeDrugs.org
Treasurer/ Dr. Mark Geier: Mark@Mercury-FreeDrugs.org
Secretary/ Dr. Paul G. King: Paul_G@Mercury-FreeDrugs.org

The Coalition for Mercury-free Drugs (CoMeD) is a non-profit group that is dedicated to reducing the mercury-exposure risks for the unborn, infants, children, adolescents, and adults. CoMeD values the right of informed consent and commits itself to requiring that this right is upheld whenever a mercury-containing drug is injected or administered to a patient at levels exceeding the applicable governmental regulatory safety guidelines. The president of CoMeD is the Reverend Lisa K. Sykes who was injected with a thimerosal-containing vaccine, without informed consent, during her 28th week of pregnancy and gave birth to a son with autism. The Geier's and CoMeD's president, Rev. Lisa K. Sykes were invited to make presentations about the deleterious effects of mercury before the second Intergovernmental Negotiating Committee (INC2) of the United Nations Environmental Programme held in Japan. Dr. Geier and his son David have also addressed Congress.

Sound Choice Pharmaceutical Institute
AVM Biotechnology
1749 Dexter Ave N
Seattle, Washington 98109
President/ Theresa A. Deisher, Ph.D.
206-906-9922
tdeisher@soundchoice.org
tdeisher@avmbiotech.com
www.soundchoice.org

Sound Choice Pharmaceutical Institute (SCPI) is a non-profit, biomedical research organization that was founded to promote consumer awareness about the widespread use of electively aborted fetal material in the discovery, development, and commercialization of pharmaceuticals. The organization's cutting edge research has also established a connection between retroviral and human fetal contaminants in vaccines and the worldwide autism epidemic. SCPI courageously stands up to the government agencies and the pharmaceutical companies who have neglected to protect our children and our basic consumer rights. The organization has an uncompromised quest for the truth, so it has great difficulties obtaining funding in the current political climate and relies solely on the donations of supporters to continue its work.

The Great Plains Laboratory Inc.
11813 W. 77th St.
Lenexa, Kansas 66214
Director/William Shaw, Ph.D.
Toll free: 800-288-0383
Fax: 913-341-6207
CustomerService@GPL4U.com
www.greatplainslaboratory.com

The Great Plains Laboratory, Inc. is a world leader in testing for nutritional factors that are involved in chronic illnesses such as autism, fibromyalgia, and Attention deficit/ hyperactivity disorder (ADHD). It also offers a variety of metabolic tests that include immune deficiency evaluations, amino acid tests, comprehensive fatty acid tests, organic acids testing, metal toxicity, and food allergies tests. Director, William Shaw, Ph.D., is board certified in the fields of clinical chemistry and toxicology by the American Board of Clinical Chemistry, and he is the author of Biological Treatments for Autism and PDD, originally published in 1998, and Autism Beyond the Basics published in 2009. He is also a frequent speaker at conferences worldwide. Dr. Shaw is the stepfather of a child with autism and has helped thousands of patients and medical practitioners to successfully improve the lives of people with autism.

Institute for Responsible Technology (IRT)
P.O Box 469
Fairfield, Iowa 52556
Phone: 641-209-1765
Fax: 1-888-386-6051
Founder: Jeffery Smith
info@responsibletechnology.org

The Institute for Responsible Technology (IRT) is a world leader in educating policy makers and the public about genetically modified (GM) foods and crops. IRT investigates and reports the risks associated with GM foods, and their impact on the environment, economy, people's health, and agriculture, as well as the problems associated with current research, regulation, corporate practices, and reporting. IRT has worked with nearly 40 countries on six continents to improve government policies and influence consumer buying habits. IRT's dedicated team of experts, consultants, and staff members generously donate their time and experience to mobilize citizens, organizations, businesses, healthcare professionals, and the media in an effort to achieve a critical mass of consumer rejection of GM foods. The organization's website has become one of the most respected resources for online videos, podcasts, blogs, and reports for accurate and up to date information on GMOs, and its "Spilling the Beans" newsletter is a trusted source of updates, events, and news.